Swarm Robotics, From Biology to Robotics

Edited by

Ester Martínez Martín

Swarm Robotics, From Biology to Robotics
Edited by Ester Martínez Martín

Republished by InTech
Janeza Trdine 9, 51000 Rijeka, Croatia

Additional hard copies can be obtained from orders@intechopen.com

Swarm Robotics, From Biology to Robotics,
Edited by Ester Martínez Martín
p. cm.
ISBN 978-953-307-075-9

For EU product safety concerns:
IN TECH d.o.o., Prolaz Marije Krucifikse Kozulić 3, 51000 Rijeka, Croatia,
info@intechopen.com or visit our website at intechopen.com.

Meet the editor

Computer Engineer and PhD from the Universitat Jaume I of Castellón. Assistant Professor Doctor in the Department of Computer Science and Artificial Intelligence. He has taught various subjects related to Artificial Intelligence, Robotics, programming and web development. Lines of work : Artificial Intelligence; robotics; image processing; visual recognition of objects

Preface

In nature, it is possible to observe a cooperative behaviour in all animals, since, according to Charles Darwin's theory, every being, from ants to human beings, form groups in which most individuals work for the common good. However, although study of dozens of social species has been done for a century, details of how and why cooperation evolved remain to be worked out. Actually, cooperative behaviour has been studied from different points of view. For instance evolutionary biologists and animal behaviour researchers look for the genetic basis and molecular drivers of this kind of behaviours, as well as the physiological, environmental, and behavioural impetus for sociality; while neuroscientists discover key correlations between brain chemicals and social strategies. From a more mathematical point of view, economics have developed a modelling approach, based on game theory, to quantify cooperation and predict behavioural outcomes under different circumstances. Although game theory has helped to reveal an apparently innate desire for fairness, developed models are still imperfect. Furthermore, social insect behaviour, from a biological point of view, might be emulated by a micro-robot colony and, in that way, analysis of a tremendous amount of insect trajectories and manual event counting is replaced by tracking several miniature robots on a desktop table.

Swarm robotics is a new approach that emerged on the field of artificial swarm intelligence, as well as the biological studies of insects (i.e. ants and other fields in nature) which coordinate their actions to accomplish tasks that are beyond the capabilities of a single individual. In particular, swarm robotics is focused on the coordination of decentralised, self-organised multi-robot systems in order to describe such a collective behaviour as a consequence of local interactions with one another and with their environment.

Research in swarm robotics involves from robot design to their controlling behaviours, by including tracking techniques for systematically studying swarm-behaviour. Moreover, swarm robotic-based techniques can be used in a number of applications. This is, for instance, the case of the Particle Swarm Optimization (PSO) which is a direct search method, based on swarm concepts, that models and predicts social behaviour in the presence of objectives. In this case, the swarm under study is typically modelled by particles in multidimensional space that have two essential reasoning capabilities: their memory of their own best position and the knowledge of the global or their neighbourhood's best, such that swarm members communicate good positions to each other and adjust their own position and velocity based on those good positions in order to obtain the best problem solution.

Different challenges have to be solved in the field of swarm robotics. This book is focused on real practical applications by analyzing how individual robotic agents should behave in a robotic swarm in order to achieve a specific goal such as target localization or path planning.

In this context, the first paper, by Hereford and Siebold, concentrates on looking for a target in a room. They describe, on the one hand, the way a PSO algorithm, based on bird flocking, may be embedded into a robot swarm; and, on the other, the implementation of a four-step trophallactic behaviour of social insects in a robotic platform by making sensor measurements instead of exchanging information when two or more particles are in contact. Different software and hardware tests were developed to evaluate both search strategy performances.

Another issue which may be solved by PSO methods is the robotic cell problem, where each integrating machine could be identified as a member of a swarm. In this context, Kamalabadi et al. present a hybrid PSO algorithm to find a schedule robot movement to minimize cycle time when multiple-type parts three-machine robotic cells are considered. Its performance has been compared with three well-known metaheuristic algorithms: Genetic Algorithm (GA), Basic Algorithm (PSO-

I) and Constriction Algorithm (PSO-II), by succeeding in the most problems, especially for large-sized ones.

The next two papers have focused on the problem of path planning for mobile robots. Firstly, Curkovic et al. introduce a way to solve the navigation problem for a robot in a workspace containing differently shaped and distributed by means of a simplification of Honey Bees Mating Algorithm. Moreover, a plan optimization technique that results in a minimization of the required time or the travelled distance is proposed. Again, method performance is successfully evaluated with respect to the Genetic Algorithm. Secondly, Xue et al. apply PSO-type control for real-time path planning on a typical swarm of wheeled mobile robots in an unstructured environment. Furthermore, an overview of a system modelling at both individual and swarm levels as well as a fusion-framework is presented. Their study was tested through virtual signal generators and simulations about swarm-component measuring and fusing.

Another application of the PSO techniques is the design of an infinite impulse response (IIR) digital filter of robot force/position sensors. Zhang proposes an IIR filter design from the knowledge of the structure of a filter and master of an intelligent optimization algorithm. The PSO algorithm is then used to optimize parameter values. Newly, simulation is used to validate the developed technique.

Finally, it is essential to systematically study and test swarm-behaviour by analyzing what each swarm member is doing as well as where and when it acts. For that purpose, Martínez and del Pobil has developed a visual application that robustly identifies and tracks all robotic swarm members. Different situations and visual systems were studied to achieve that goal. Experimental results on a real system are also presented.

This book has only provided a partial picture of the field of swarm robotics by focusing on practical applications. The global assessment of the contributions contained in this book is reasonably positive since they highlighted that it is necessary to adapt and remodel biological strategies to cope with the added complexity and problems that arise when robot individuals are considered.

Ester Martínez Martín

Contents

1

Bio-inspired search strategies for robot swarms

James M. Hereford and Michael A. Siebold
Murray State University, Murray, KY
USA

1. Introduction

Our goal is as follows: build a suite/swarm of (very) small robots that can search a room for a "target". We envision that the robots will be about the size of a quarter dollar, or smaller, and have a sensor or sensors that "sniff" out the desired target. For example, the target could be a bomb and the robot sensors would be a chemical detectors that can distinguish the bomb from its surroundings. Or the target could be a radiation leak and the sensors would be radiation detectors. In each search scenario, we assume that the target gives off a diffuse residue that can be detected with a sensor.

It is not very efficient to have the suite of robots looking randomly around the room hoping to "get lucky" and find the target. There needs to be some way to coordinate the movements of the many robots. There needs to be an algorithm that can guide the robots toward promising regions to search while not getting distracted by local variations. The search algorithm must have the following constraints:

- The search algorithm should be distributed among the many robots. If the algorithm is located in one robot, then the system will fail if that robot fails.
- The search algorithm should be computationally simple. The processor on each bot is small, has limited memory, and there is a limited power source (a battery) so the processor needs to be power efficient. Therefore, the processor will be a simple processor.
- The algorithm needs to be scalable from one robot up to 10's, 100's, even 1000's of robots. The upper limit on the number of robots will be set by the communication links among the robots; there needs to be a way to share information among the robots without requiring lots of communication traffic.
- The search algorithm must allow for contiguous movement of the robots.

This chapter will describe two search strategies for robot swarms that are based on biological systems. The first search strategy is based on the flocking behavior of birds and fishes. This flocking behavior is the inspiration behind the Particle Swarm Optimization (PSO) algorithm that has been used in software for many types of optimization problems. In the PSO algorithm the potential solutions, called particles, "fly" through the problem space by following some simple rules. All of the particles have a fitness value based on the value or measurement at the particle's position and have velocities which direct the flight of the particles. The velocity of each particle is updated based on the particle's current velocity as well as the best fitness of any particle in the group.

We describe how the PSO algorithm can be embedded into a robot swarm by letting each bot's behavior be like a particle in the PSO. We call the algorithm the physically embedded PSO (pePSO). The bots swarm throughout the search space and take measurements. Over time, they cluster near the peak(s) or targets. We show through both 2D simulation results and robot hardware results that the pePSO effectively finds the targets with a minimum number of bot-bot communications.

The second search strategy is based on the trophallactic behavior of social insects. Trophallaxis is the exchange of fluid by direct mouth-to-mouth contact. This phenomenon is observed in ants, bees, wasps and even dogs and birds. In our trophallaxis-based algorithm, the bots do not actually exchange information but instead make sensor measurements when two or more bots/particles are "in contact". The bots remain stationary for a certain time that is proportional to the measurement value. Bots thus cluster in areas of the search space that have high fitness/measurement values.

This new trophallaxis-based search algorithm has several advantages over other swarm-based search techniques. First, no bot-bot communication is required. Thus, there is no concern with communication radius, protocol, or bandwidth. Second, the bots do not have to know their position. During the search, the bot/particle moves randomly except when it collides and stops, takes a measurement, and waits. At the end of the search, the cluster locations can be determined from a remote camera, special-purpose robot, or human canvassing.

This paper is organized as follows: section 2 gives background on the Particle Swarm Optimization algorithm and its use in robot swarms and section 3 gives results from simulations and hardware results of embedding the PSO into a robot swarm. Section 4 discusses the trophallaxis- based search algorithm and section 5 gives simulation results using the trophallaxis algorithm. In section 6 we give our conclusions.

2. Particle Swarm Optimization and robots

In Particle Swarm Optimization (PSO) (Eberhart & Kennedy, 1995; Clerc &Kennedy, 2002; Eberhart & Shi, 2004), the potential solutions, called particles, "fly" through the problem space by following some simple rules. All of the particles have fitness values based on their position and have velocities which direct the flight of the particles. PSO is initialized with a group of random particles (solutions), and then searches for optima by updating generations. In every iteration, each particle is updated by following two "best" values. The first one is the best solution (fitness) the particle has achieved so far. This value is called pbest. Another "best" value that is tracked by the particle swarm optimizer is the best value obtained so far by any particle within the neighborhood. This best value is a neighborhood or local best and called lbest.

After finding the two best values, the particle updates its velocity and positions with following equations:

$$v_{n+1} = w_i v_n + c1 * r1 * (pbest_n - p_n) + c2 * r2 * (lbest_n - p_n) \tag{1}$$

$$p_{n+1} = p_n + v_{n+1} \tag{2}$$

w_i is the inertia coefficient which slows velocity over time; v_n is the current particle velocity;

p_n is the current particle position in the search space; r1 and r2 are random numbers between (0,1); c1 and c2 are learning factors. The stop condition is usually the maximum number of allowed iterations for PSO to execute or the minimum error requirement.

Because of the required search algorithm characteristics listed in section 1, we chose the PSO as the starting point for the search control algorithm. The PSO is computationally simple. It requires only four multiplies and four add/subtracts to update the velocity and then one add to update the position. The PSO can also be a distributed algorithm. Each agent/particle/bot can update its own velocity and position. The only external information is the local best - the best value by any particle within the neighborhood. The calculation of the local best can be done with a simple comparative statement. Thus, each bot does not need to know the results from each member of the population as in many traditional schemes. (Though in some versions of the PSO, the lbest is replaced by gbest, the global best - the best value of any particle within the population.)

The PSO also allows the contiguous movement of the bots. The updated position is relative to the current position so there are no jump changes in position or random movements. If there are constraints on the movement of the bot during each iteration, then limitations can be placed on the maximum and minimum velocity that is allowed for each particle/bot.

We propose embedding the PSO into a swarm of robots. In our approach, each bot is behaves as one particle in the PSO. Thus, each bot moves based on the PSO update equations (eqs. 1 and 2), makes a measurement and then broadcasts to the other bots in the swarm if it finds a new lbest measurement. We make some slight changes to the classic PSO algorithm to make it work with a robot swarm, so we call our algorithm the physically-embedded PSO (pePSO).

Other authors have investigated using biological principles (Zarzhitsky & Spears, 2005; Valdastri et al., 2006; Schmickl & Crailsheim, 2006; Triannni et al., 2006) and PSO-type algorithms (Hayes et al., 2000; Hayes et al., 2002, Doctor et al., 2004; Pugh & Martinoli, 2006; Pugh & Martinoli, 2007; Jatmiko et al., 2006; Jatmiko et al., 2007) with multiple (simple) robots for search applications. Specifically, Hayes et al. report using autonomous mobile robots for beacon localization (Hayes et al., 2000) and plume tracking/odor source localization (Hayes et al., 2002); they base their search techniques on biological principles (surge "upwind") but do not use the PSO algorithm directly. Doctor et al. (Doctor et al., 2004) discuss using the PSO for multiple robot searches. Their focus is on optimizing the parameters of the search PSO and do not consider the scalability of the standard PSO to large numbers of robots.

There are at least three other research groups that have investigated using mobile robots to do searches under the control of a PSO algorithm. Pugh et al. (Pugh & Martinoli, 2006; Pugh & Martinoli, 2007), explored using PSO on problems in noisy environments, focusing on unsupervised robotic learning. They used the PSO to evolve a robot controller that avoids obstacles and finds the source. They also investigated the possibility of using PSO without global position information. Jatmiko et al. (Jatmiko et al., 2006; Jatmiko et al., 2007) used mobile robots for plume detection and traversal. They utilized a modified form of the PSO to control the robots and consider how the robots respond to search space changes such as turbulence and wind changes. Akat and Gazi (Akat and Gazi, 2008) propose a version of the PSO for robot swarms that uses dynamic neighborhoods and asynchronous updates.

3. pePSO results

3.1 Simulation Conditions

We simulated the pePSO using three different test functions and five different target points with each function. The five different target points are shown in Figure 1. Only one target point was active during each simulation run; that is, there is only one target value in the search space at a time.

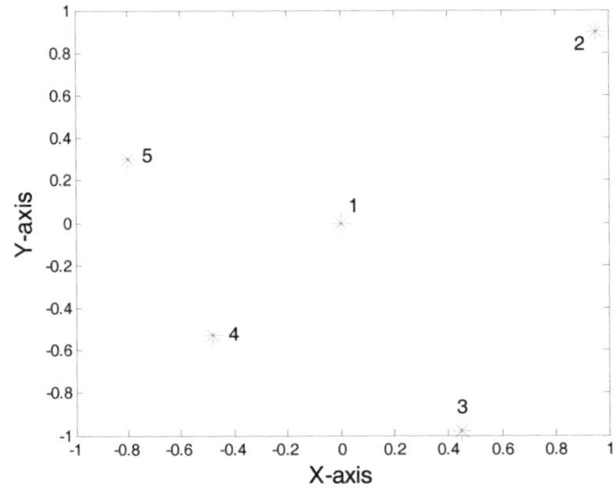

Fig. 1. Map of simulation search space scaled to cover -1 to +1 and showing the 5 different target point locations.

The three functions used in the simulation were the parabolic/spherical function, Rastrigin function, and Rosenbrock function. The three test functions are given by:

parabolic/spherical:

$$f(x,y) = (x - x_{target})^2 + (y - y_{target})^2 \tag{3}$$

Rastrigin:

$$f(x,y) = (x - x_{target})^2 - 10\cos(2\pi(x - x_{target})) + 10) + (y - y_{target})^2 - 10\cos(2\pi(y - y_{target})) + 10) \tag{4}$$

Rosenbrock:

$$f(x,y) = (1 - (x - x_{target} + 1))^2 + 100((y - y_{target} + 1) - (x - x_{target} + 1)^2)^2 \tag{5}$$

where (x,y) is the position of the bot/particle and (x_{target}, y_{target}) is the position of the target point. The spherical function was chosen because it approximates the expected dissipation pattern of chemicals, heat, etc that would be emitted by real-world targets. The Rastrigin and Rosenbrock functions were chosen because they are commonly used functions in PSO testing and they approximate a search space with obstacles and undulations. The Rosenbrock function used in our simulations is slightly different than the one reported in other simulations. We have shifted the minimum value of the function to the target location instead of offset by (1,1) in x and y. This ensures that the target point is within the search space.

Plots of the three test functions are shown in Figure 2. In each case, we are trying to find the location of the global minimum. The size of the search spaces were -100 to 100 for the parabolic function and -5.1 to 5.1 for the Rastrigin and Rosenbrock functions. (The dimensions correspond roughly to meters as we set the velocity on the bot based on meters per second.) Unlike most PSO simulations, the search space boundary for our simulations represents a "hard" border - the particles/bots can not go outside the search space. We use a hard border because we want to approximate the conditions of actual robots searching in a room or some other confined space. The target point locations shown in Figure 1 were scaled for each of the search spaces. The (x,y) target locations are given in Table 1.

Target point	Parabolic	Rastrigin/ Rosenbrock
1	(0,0)	(0,0)
2	(94.7, 90.0)	(4.86, 4.61)
3	(45.1, -98.5)	(2.3, -5.02)
4	(-48.0, -52.7)	(-2.46, -2.71)
5	(-79.6, 29.9)	(-4.1, 1.54)

Table 1. Target Locations for each of the three Test Functions

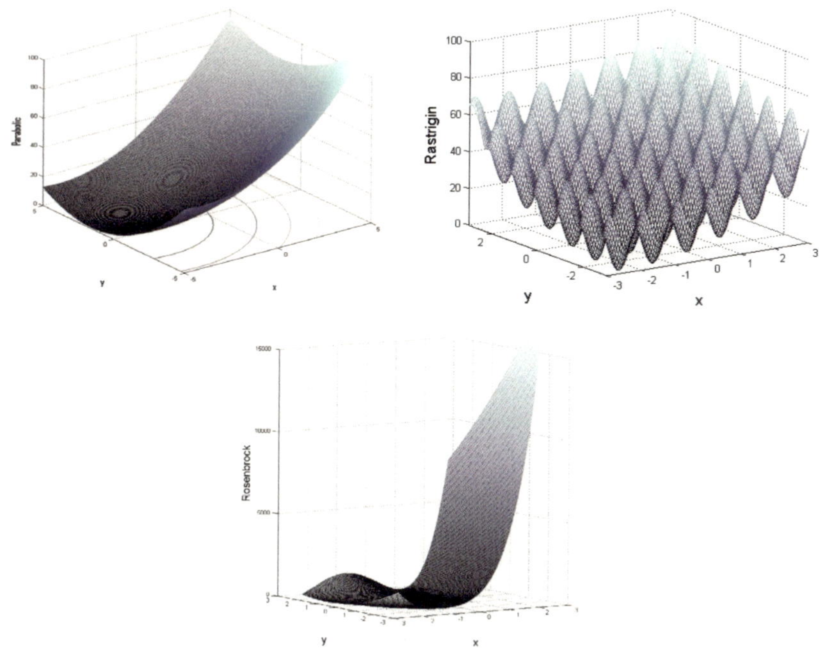

Fig. 2. Plots of three test functions. (a) Parabolic function with contours. Min value (the target value) is at [-4.1 1.54]; (b) Rastrigin function with min (target) point at -2.46 -2.71; (b) Rosenbrock function with target point = [0 0]. Min value is at a saddle point.

The simulation incorporated the mobility limitations of our small robots. The max turning radius allowed was 36 degrees and the maximum velocity was 0.9 m/s. The bots were positioned randomly around the search space at t = 0. In our expected deployment scenario the bots will most likely be "dropped off" at a particular point (e.g., near a door or window) and not dispersed randomly about the search space. However, we can easily incorporate a dispersion algorithm (Hsiang et al. 2002; Morlok & Gini, 2004) to spread the bots throughout the search space before beginning the search phase using pePSO.
For the simulation results, we used the following parameter values. Inertia coefficient, w_i, was set to 0.9. The max velocity of the bots was set to 0.9 m/s. Note that this is different than the old Vmax parameter in the original version of the PSO. We set an initial v for each bot/particle to simulate the behavior of the physical robot. The c1 and c2 coefficients were both set to 2.1. Since only three bots were used, the lbest topology was the same as gbest. That is, all of the bots communicated gbest and gbest location with all of the other bots.
One major difference between our simulations and the PSO results reported in the literature is how we calculate a successful search, and, relatedly, the stop condition. A successful search occurred when a bot/particle got within a tolerance of 0.2 in the x and y dimensions of the target location. Most PSO researchers track function value but we used location because of our search application. The simulation stopped when a bot got near the target or when 5400 function evaluations (about 15 minuntes) elapsed. Compared to other results, 5400 is a relatively small number of function evaluations but we want the bots to find the target within a reasonable time period.

3.2 Simulation results

To evaluate the effectiveness of the pePSO, we made several simulation runs. An effective "hit" occurred when one of the bots found the global peak within 15 minutes of simulation time (5400 function iterations). We used the 5 different target points and did 200 test cases for each target point for a total of 1000 runs for each test function. In each test case, the initial start locations of the bots were different. We evaluated the overall effectiveness of the algorithm (i.e., how many times it found the "target") and compared the pePSO to the standard PSO. In tables 2, 3 and 4 we compare the pePSO to the standard PSO with the number of particles set to 3. We modified the standard PSO to calculate the percent found (number of hits) based on proximity to the target location rather than on the function value so that it was consistent with the pePSO. The tables report the percentage of targets found. The results are shown for each of the three test functions as well as the total for all five target points.
For all three test functions, the pePSO performed much better than the PSO using same number of particles.

	Target point 1	Target point 2	Target point 3	Target point 4	Target point 5	Total
PSO	100	38.5	51	98	90.5	75.6
pePSO	99.5	99.5	99.5	99.5	100	**99.6**

Table 2. Parabolic Function, Results show the percent of targets found (out of 200 searches) for each of the five target points and also the overall results.

	Target point 1	Target point 2	Target point 3	Target point 4	Target point 5	Total
PSO	31	33.5	48	26	19	31.5
pePSO	97.5	96.5	65.5	99.5	92	**90.2**

Table 3. Rastrigin Function. Results show the percent of targets foune (out of 200 searches) for each of the five target points and also the overall results.

	Target point 1	Target point 2	Target point 3	Target point 4	Target point 5	Total
PSO	75	53	29.5	51.5	45	50.8
pePSO	86.5	92	55.5	88.5	92	**82.9**

Table 4. Rosenbrock Function. Results show the percent of targets foune (out of 200 searches) for each of the five target points and also the overall results.

The results in Tables 2-4 show that none of the algorithms found the target location 100% of the time, even with a relatively easy problem like the parabolic function. There are a number of reasons for the missed detections. First, we declared a failed search after relatively few function evaluations (relative compared to other researchers' results); we limited both the standard PSO and the pePSO to 5400 function evaluations. Second, we are not using very many particles/bots. Third, we have placed some of the target locations at positions near the edge of the search space which makes it somewhat more difficult for the PSO to find them.

3.3 Hardware test conditions

To investigate the effectiveness of the pePSO algorithm, we did several hardware experiments. In the experiments, a diffuse light source was placed near the ceiling of a dark room and pointed downward. Bots with light sensors were placed at various starting positions about 2 m apart to see (a) how often and (b) how quickly they could find the brightest spot of light in the room.

The layout of the test area is shown in Figure 3. The hatched boxes in the middle represent the obstacles that we placed in the search space for the second half of the testing. The highest concentration of light is immediately to the left of the vertical obstacle. Since we are using a diffuse light source, the global best is actually a rectangle approximately .25 m by .3 m.

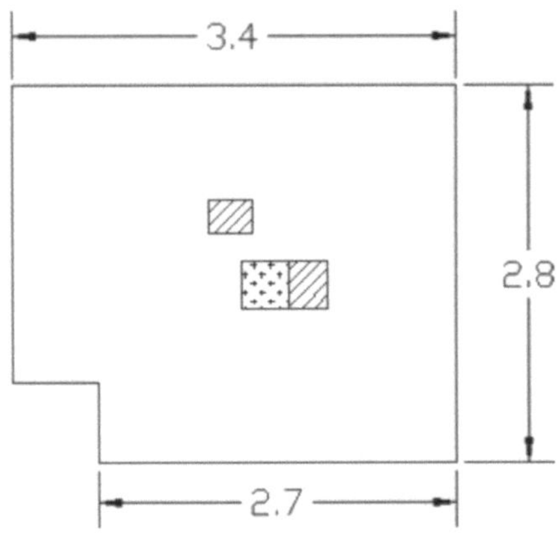

Fig. 3. Graphical representation of test area. Dimensions shown are in meters. Figure shows two obstacles and starred area is location of peak light intensity.

To make the pePSO work in a robotic swarm, we had to make several adjustments. First, the bots determine their position by triangulating from three cricket motes set up as beacons. To correct for any missed packets, the bots are programmed to move to the next position and then wait for two consecutive "clean" measurements (distance measurements within 2 cm of each other) from all three beacons. This wait leads to relatively long search times.

A second adjustment had to be made because of mechanical limitations in each bot. Since the bots steer with the front two wheels, the bots move in arcs rather than straight lines (see Figure 4). Each bot moves toward the desired position in the search space but upon arrival at the destination point, the orientation of the bot, as given by the direction of the wheels, is usually skewed relative to the movement. To compensate, we updated the bot's orientation angle at each iteration based on the bot's current position and its previous position. This eliminates the buildup of orientation errors that occur when a strict dead reckoning system for orientation is used.

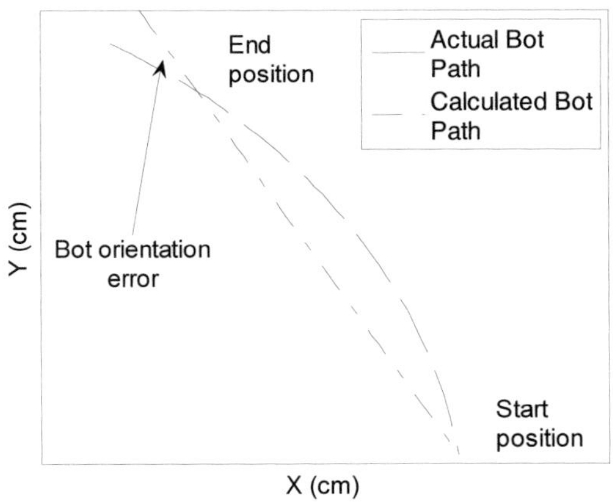

Fig. 4. Illustration of bot orientation mismatch.

A third adjustment was required because of the size of the bots. Unlike a simulation-only PSO, the hardware bots can get "stuck" at an obstacle or collide with another bot (particle). Once a bot got stuck or collided, we programmed the bot to back up and turn right. This allows the bot to move around long obstacles, such as a wall, even though it may require more than one cycle of backing up and turning to avoid.

3.4 Hardware results

During the hardware experiments, we programmed each bot in the swarm with identical programs. (The only difference is that each bot has a different identification number.) The PSO parameters used were c1 = 2, c2 = 2, and $w_i = 1.0$. We tried using $w_i = 0.8$ but it slowed the bots down considerably and led to many failed searches. Each bot was programmed to move in the desired direction for approximately 0.5 sec. The bot would then make a measurement, determine its new position, calculate its desired movement direction based on the PSO update, orient its wheels to that direction, if possible, and then move for 0.5 sec. The search was ended when there had been 20 iterations of the algorithm with no new local best discovered. We made some test runs using a stop condition with 10 iterations with no new lbest but we determined that 10 was insufficient.

Figure 5 shows the path traced out by 1 bot during a search sequence. The x and y axes are to scale and the axes are in cm. The asterisks (*) marks in the figures represent positions where a new local best was found. The rectangular box is the peak area of the search space. The bot starts in lower right corner. It moves up (north), finds new lbests and continues upward. When it starts to move away from the peak, it circles clockwise and then begins moving to the left (westward). When the light intensity measurements begin to taper off again, the bot circles counterclockwise back toward its previous best. The circle behavior is because the bot is limited in its turning radius - it can not make a sharp turn. Thus, it must move toward the global best in a roundabout fashion. Eventually, it settles on to the peak light value.

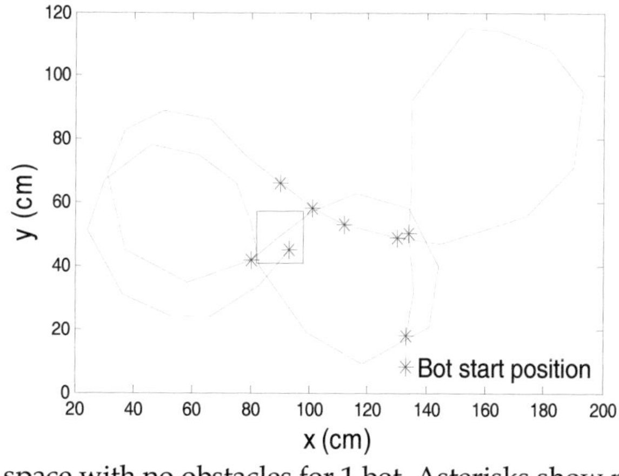

Fig. 5. Path in search space with no obstacles for 1 bot. Asterisks show positions where lbests were recorded.

The PSO algorithm was tested using swarm sizes of 1, 2 and 3 bots. (The 1-bot swarm was merely for baseline comparison.) Ten runs were made for each of the three cases. We tracked how many times the bots found the brightest spot and how long it took for the bots to locate the peak. If twenty iterations of the algorithm passed with no new global best, then we declare the search is over.

The quantitative results are shown in Tables 5 and 6. The results are for two different search spaces: one with no obstacles and one with obstacles. The table shows the number of bots in the swarm, the number of successful (completed) runs, the median search time for all searches, the average search time for just the successful searches, the standard deviation of the successful search times and the 90% confidence interval for the average time. The confidence interval is based on t-statistics using the successful searches as the degrees of freedom.

Runs without obstacles.

Test condition	Complete runs (out of 10)	Median time (sec)	Average (sec)	Standard deviation (sec)	Confidence Interval (90%)
pePSO (1 bot)	6	118.5	180.2	101	± 83.1
pePSO (2 bots)	10	177	176.1	68.9	± 39.9
pePSO (3 bots)	10	133.5	109.6	55.0	± 31.9
Phototaxis (1 bot)	9	280	273.8	45.1	± 28.0
3 bot (no commun)	10	351.5	362.7	98.7	± 57.2

Table 5. Results from using PSO to program a suite of bots with sensor and position corrections. No obstacles in the search space

Test condition	Complete runs (out of 10)	Median time (sec)	Average (sec)	Standard deviation (sec)	Confidence Interval (90%)
pePSO (1 bot)	8	268	250.2	108.6	± 71.4
pePSO (2 bots)	10	178	181.7	76.1	± 44.1
pePSO (3 bots)	10	108.5	125.8	65.2	± 37.8
3 bot (no commun)	9	290	294.1	111.3	± 69.0

Table 6. Results from pePSO in a search space with obstacles

Table 5 also shows the results from searches using a phototaxis approach and using three bots without any communication among the bots. These experiments provide a comparison for the effectiveness and search times for the pePSO. For the phototaxis experiments, we used a cylinder to make a directional light sensor on one of the bots. The bot then took light intensity measurements as it made a 360 degree loop. (The loop had a radius of 0.25 m.) The bot then moved in the direction of the greatest light reading. Our test results show that the multi-bot pePSO is faster and more effective than the phototaxis approach.

To compare the effectiveness of the multi-bot pePSO, we did a 3 bot search with no communication among the bots. Essentially, each bot moved toward bright regions of the room based on the PSO update equation without the lbest term. If a bot received a higher light reading than ever before, then it continued moving in that direction; thus, it is a pseudo-gradient method. The results in Table 6 show that the 3-bot pseudo-gradient method was effective (19 out of 20 successful runs) but it was much slower than the 3-bot pePSO. The 3-bot pePSO search is over 55% faster than the pseudo-gradient based 3-bot search both with obstacles and without obstacles.

Increasing the number of bots does two things. It leads to more successful searches and reduces the time to find the peak/best value. We see that even with the obstacles in the search space, the swarm is still able to find the "target" or peak light intensity every time for a multi-bot search. In general, the searches take longer when there are obstacles in the search space but the search is still successful. The times should be used for comparison purposes and not necessarily as an absolute reference. As mentioned earlier, sketchy communications with the beacons forced the bots to wait for two consecutive good data points at each iteration. This waiting time greatly increased the search time.

To overcome the weak signal from one of the beacons, we modified the position algorithm to allow the bot to calculate its position with distance data from only two beacons. The bot initially tried to get two consecutive good measurements from all three beacons. If after seven seconds there was still not accurate distance information, then the bot would use the distance measurements from two beacons to calculate its (x,y) position.

During our initial experiments, we noticed that the light sensors on the bots were mismatched. That is, different bots would read different values for the same light level. This imbalance led to some erroneous values for the search times. Specifically, if the bot with the lowest light readings found the peak value first, then other bots would circle toward that point. When another bot (with a light sensor that recorded higher light values) moved to the same location, it would record a higher light value and the algorithm would think a "new" target had been found. To correct for the different sensor readings, we used linear splines for each individual sensor to adjust and match the light sensor outputs of the three bots.

4. Trophallaxis and robots

4.1 Background

In our trophallaxis-based algorithm, the bots (or, more generally, particles) do not actually exchange information but instead make sensor measurements when two or more bots/particles are "in contact". The bots remain stationary for a certain time that is proportional to the measurement value. Bots thus cluster in areas of the search space that have high fitness/measurement values. Each bot is independent (i.e., not reliant on neighbor bot measurements) but must have contact with the other bots to find the peaks.

This new trophallaxis-based search algorithm has several advantages over other swarm-based search techniques. First, no bot-bot (particle-particle) communication is required. Thus, there is no concern with communication radius, protocol, or bandwidth. Unlike classic PSO-based techniques, the bots do not have to be arranged in topologies or communicate personal or global best information to any neighbors. The only communication that may be required is signaling between bots to differentiate collisions between bots and collisions with obstacles.

Second, the bots do not have to know their position. If position information is available, from beacons or some other source, then position information can be communicated at the end of the search. But during the search, the bot/particle moves randomly except when it stops, takes a measurement, and waits. At the end of the search, the cluster locations can be determined from a remote camera, special-purpose robot, or human canvassing.

Third, no on-board processing or memory is required - the bot does not even have to do the relatively simple PSO update equations. The bot/particle moves at random, takes a measurement and does a multiplication. It is so simple that a microcontroller may not be required, only some simple digital logic hardware.

The Trophallactic Cluster Algorithm (TCA) has four basic steps:

Step 1: Bots start randomly throughout the search space and then move at random through the search space.

Step 2: If a bot intersects or collides with another bot, then it stops.

Step 3: After stopping, the bot measures the "fitness" or function value at that point in space. It then waits at that point for a prescribed time based on the measurement. The higher the measurement value, then the longer the wait time.

Step 4: When done, determine the locations of the clusters of bots. (We assume that this step is performed by an agent or agents that are separate from the swarm.)

Step 1 is similar to the first step in the standard Particle Swarm Optimization (PSO) algorithm. For a software only optimization scheme, it is straightforward to randomly initialize the particles within the search boundaries. For a hardware scheme, a dispersion algorithm (Siebold & Hereford 2008; Spears et al., 2006) can be used to randomly place the bots.

For random movement, we pick a direction and then have the bots move in a straight line in that direction until they encounter an obstacle, boundary or other bot. Thus, there is no path adjustment or Brownian motion type movement once the (random) initial direction is set. There is a maximum velocity at which the bots move throughout the search space. We experimented briefly with different maximum velocities to see its affect on overall results but we usually set it based on the expected maximum velocity of our hardware bots.

In step 2, we detect collision by determining whether bots are within a certain distance of each other. In software, this is done after each time step. In hardware, it can be done using infrared sensors on each bot.

In a hardware implementation of the TCA, we would need to distinguish between collisions with obstacles and collisions with other bots. Obstacles and walls just cause the bot/particle to reorient and move in a new direction. They do not lead to a stop/measure/wait sequence. So once a collision is detected, the bot would have to determine if the collision is with another bot or with an obstacle. One way to do this is to have the bots signal with LEDS (ala trophallaxis where only neighbors next to each other can exchange info). In this way, each bot will know it has encountered another bot.

Once a bot is stopped (as a result of a collision with another bot), then it measures the value of the function at that location. (In hardware, the bot would take a sensor reading.) Since the bots are nearly co-located, the function value will be nearly the same for both bots. The wait time is a multiple of the function value so the bot(s) will wait longer in areas of high fitness relative to areas with low function values. Other bots may also "collide" with the stopped and waiting bots but that will not reset the wait times for the stopped bots. For the results in this paper the wait time was exponentially related to the measurement value; we experimented with linear wait times as well.

We did step 4 (determine the clusters) when the search is "done". In general, the bots begin to collide/stop/wait at the beginning. Thus, the bots tend to cluster soon after the search begins so the search can be stopped at any time to observe the location(s) of the clusters. In 2D, the clusters tend to become more pronounced as the iterations increase so waiting a longer time can make the position(s) of the peak(s) more obvious.

4.2 Related work

The TCA is based on the work of Thomas Schmickl and Karl Crailsheim (Schmickl & Crailsheim 2006; Schmickl & Crailsheim 2008) who developed the concept based on the trophallactic behavior of honey bees. Schmickl and Crailsheim use the trophallactic concept to have a swarm of bots move (simulated) dirt from a source point to a dump point. The bots can upload "nectar" from the source point, where the amount of nectar for each bot is stored in an internal variable. As the robots move, the amount of stored nectar decreases, so the higher the nectar level, then the closer to the source. Each robot also queries the nectar level of the robots in the local neighborhood and can use this information to navigate uphill in the gradient. There is a also a dump area where the loaded robots aggregate and drop the "dirt" particles. The swarm had to navigate between the source and the dump and achieved this by establishing two distinct gradients in parallel.

Their preliminary results showed a problem where the bots tended to aggregate near the dump and the source. When that happened, the bridge or gradient information between the source and the dump was lost. To prevent the aggregation, they prevented a percentage of their robots from moving uphill and just performed a random walk with obstacle avoidance. Even though the work of Schmickl and Crailsheim is significant, they show no published results where they apply the trophallactic concept to strictly search/optimization type problems. Nor do they show results when there is more than one peak (or source point) in the search space. They also require bot-bot communications to form the pseudo-gradient that the loaded (or empty) bots follow, while our TCA approach does not require adjacent particles/bots to exchange nectar levels (or any other measured values).

In (Ngo & Schioler, 2008), Ngo and Schioler model a group of autonomous mobile robots with the possibility of self-refueling. Inspired by the natural concept of trophallaxis, they investigate a system of multiple robots that is capable of energy sharing to sustain robot life. Energy (via the exchange of rechargeable batteries) is transferred by direct contact with other robots and fixed docking stations.

In this research, we are applying the concept of trophallaxis to solve a completely different type of problem than Ngo and Schioler, though some of their results may be applicable if we expand our research to include energy use by the robots.

5. Trophallaxis search results

5.1 Test conditions

We tested the TCA algorithm on three functions: two 1D and one 2D. The 1D functions are denoted F3 and F4 and were used by Parrott and Li (Parrott and Li, 2006) for testing PSO-based algorithms that find multiple peaks in the search space. The equations for F3 and F4 are given by

$$F3(x) = \sin^6(5\pi(x^{3/4} - 0.05)) \tag{6}$$

$$F4(x) = \exp(-2\log(2)(\frac{x - 0.08}{.854})^2)\sin^6(5\pi(x^{3/4} - 0.05)) \tag{7}$$

Plots for the function F3 and F4 are shown in figure 6. Each 1D test function is defined over the scale of $0 \le x \le 1$. F3 has five equal-height peaks (global optima) that are unevenly spaced in the search space. F4 also has five unevenly spaced peaks but only one is a global optimum while the other four peaks are local optima. Our goal is to find all five peaks; that is, the global optimum plus the local optima. The peak locations are given in Table 7.

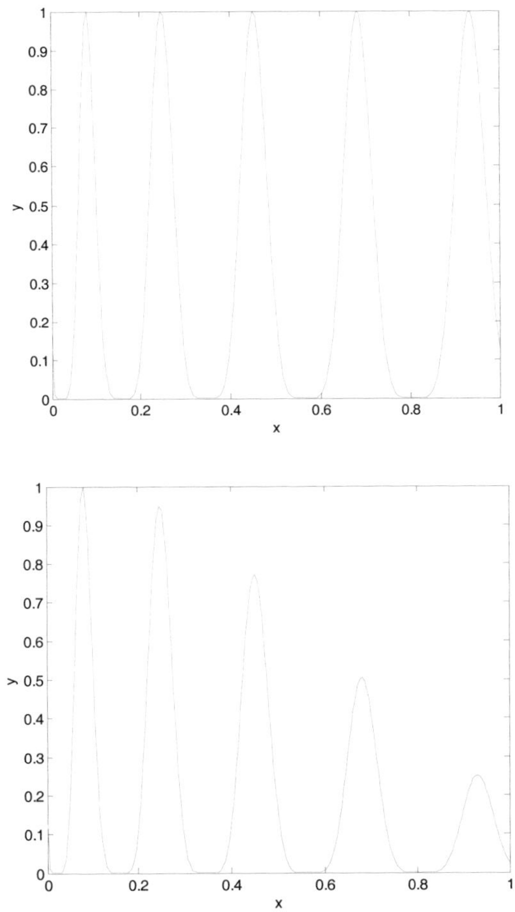

Fig. 6. 1D test function with equal peaks, F3, and with unequal peaks, F4

Peak #	1	2	3	4	5
X locations	.0797	.2465	.4505	.6815	.9340

Table 7. Peak locations for test functions F3 and F4

The 2D function is a slight variation of the standard Rastrigin function. The equation for the Rastrigin is given in equation 4 with the range on x and y is -5.12 to 5.12. The Rastrigin is highly multimodal (see figure 2) and has one global minimum. For the TCA simulations, we modified the Rastrigin so that it has a peak of 1 at (.35, .35) instead of a minimum at the origin. We also scaled the function slightly so that there are nine peaks (1 global, 8 local) within the [-5.12, 5.12] range. The modified Rastrigin function is shown in figure 7.

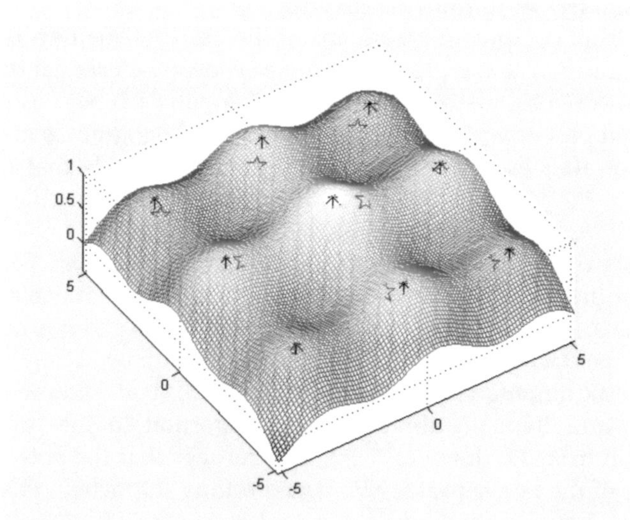

Fig. 7. Plot of modified Rastrigin function scaled so that it has 9 peaks in [-5.12,5.12] range and peak value is equal to 1.

We evaluated the effectiveness of the TCA algorithm using two different metrics. The first metric is the total percentage of peaks found (*found rate*). Since each function has multiple peaks (both global and local) we totaled the number of actual peaks that the swarm found divided by the total number of peaks (see equation 8). Note that "peaks found" refers to only those bot clusters that are within ± .04 (1D) or a radius of .4 (2D) of the actual peak location.

Found rate = (peaks found)/(total number of peaks in search space) (8)

The second metric is related to the success rate from Parrott and Li:

Success rate = (Runs where more than half of total peaks found)/(total number of runs) (9)

The *success rate* gives an indication of how many of the runs were successful. We designate a successful run as one where a majority of the peaks (more than half) in the search space are found. This definition is based on the robot search idea where the goal is for the robots to quickly cluster near the target points. We note that this is a slightly different definition for success rate than Parrott and Li; their success rate is based on the closest particle and finding all of the peaks in the search space.

The locations of the bot clusters were determined using the K-means clustering algorithm. The K-means algorithm minimizes the sum, over all clusters, of the point-to-cluster centroid distances. We then compared the cluster centroid to the actual peak location to determine if the peak was found or not. For the 1D functions, we used a tolerance of ± 0.04 between the cluster centroid and the actual peak and for the 2D functions we used a radius of 0.4.

We considered two clustering approaches; the first one uses all of the bots when determining the cluster centroids. The second approach uses only the final position of the bots that are stopped (that is, in a collision) when determining clusters. We refer to the second approach as "cluster reduction", since it reduces the number of bots that are considered.

5.2 Trophallactic Cluster Algorithm 1D results

Qualitative results from computer simulations of the TCA for the two 1D functions F3 and F4 are shown in Figure 8. The top plot in the figure shows the original function; the middle plot shows the final bot positions (after 400 iterations) with each bot position represented by a star (*). The bottom plot is a normalized histogram; the histogram is made by tracking the position of each bot after each time interval. The figure reveals that the bots do cluster around the peaks in the function and thus give evidence that the TCA will reliably find multiple peaks.

The histogram plots reveal some interesting information. For both F3 and F4, there are significant peaks in the histogram at the same locations as the function peaks, providing evidence that the bots spend a majority of time near the peaks and it is not just at the end of the simulation that the bots cluster. Also, for F3 the histogram peaks have approximately the same amplitude (peak amplitudes range from 0.7 to 1.0). For F4, however, the histogram peaks diminish in amplitude in almost direct proportion to the function peaks (peak amplitudes diminish from 1.0 down to 0.25). This implies that the bots are spending more time in the vicinity of the larger peaks. The bots are thus "attracted" to stronger signals, as expected.

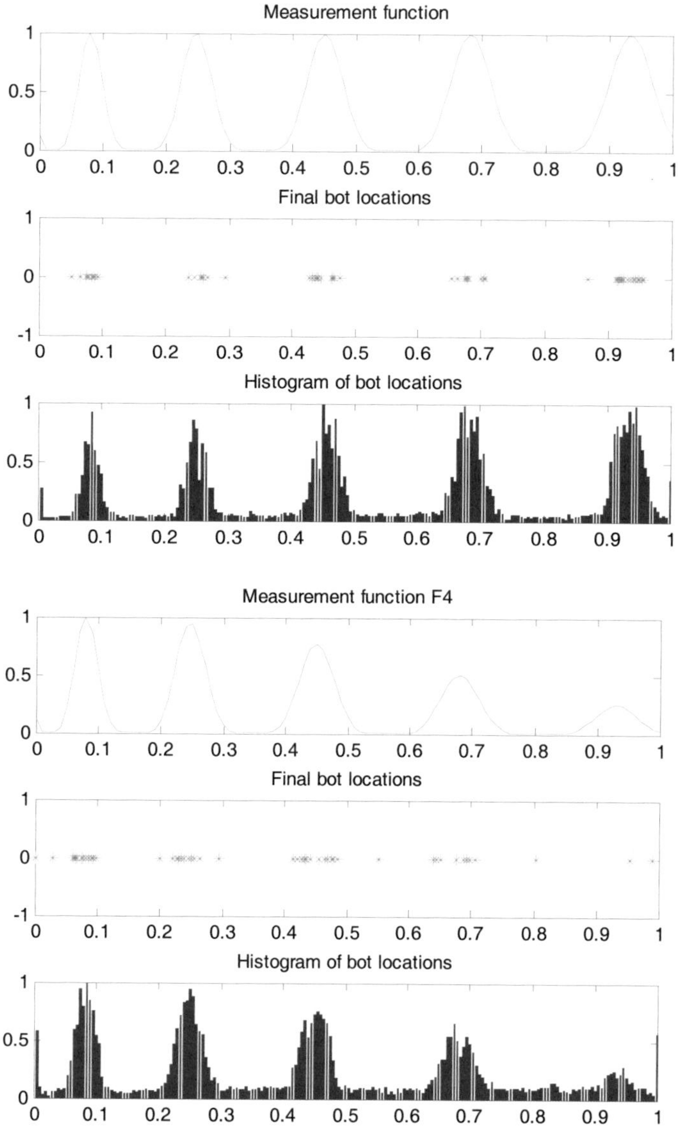

Fig. 8. Qualitative results for function F3 (left) and function F4 (right). Final bot locations are shown in the middle plot and histograms of bot positions are shown in the bottom plot

We performed computer simulations to tailor three of the parameters of TCA algorithm for 1D functions. The three parameters were *tmax*, the maximum number of iterations for the simulation, *nbots*, the number of bots to use, and *waitfactor*. The *waitfactor* sets how long each bot waits based on the measured value after a collision. We tried linear wait functions (wait time increases linearly with measurement value) but had more success with exponential wait functions give by

$$\text{Wait time} = waitfactor * (e^{(\text{measurement})}-1) \quad (11)$$

For the parameter selection, we varied one parameter at a time and repeated the simulation 100 times. Plots of the average found rate for parameters *nbots* and *waitfactor* with no cluster reduction are shown in Figure 9. The first plot shows the found rate as *nbots* is varied from 10 to 200 with *tmax* set to 500 and *waitfactor* set to 5. The second plot shows the found rate as *waitfactor* is varied from 1 to 10 with *tmax* = 500 and *nbots* = 80. Similar tests were done with cluster reduction.

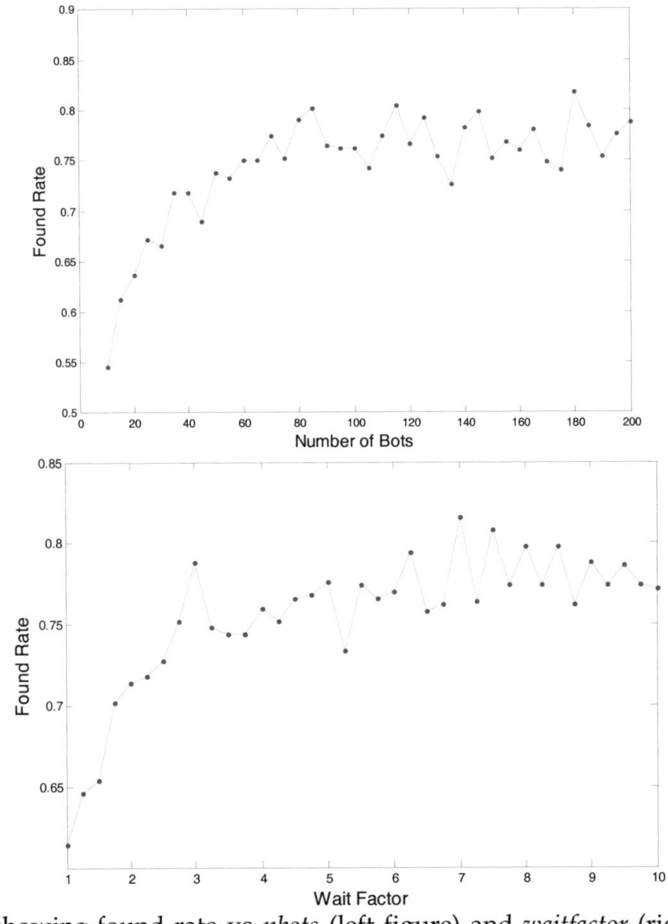

Fig. 9. Results showing found rate vs *nbots* (left figure) and *waitfactor* (right figure) for F3 function

When the peaks were found with no cluster reduction, the found rate versus the parameter value curve resembled ($1\text{-}e^{-x}$) shape and asymptotically approached a found rate of about 78%. Thus, there was not one precise parameter value but a range of parameter values that led to the best performance: *nbots* greater than 80 and *waitfactor* greater than 3. The *tmax* curve was flat - it appears that the bots quickly cluster near the peaks and there is little change in performance as the *tmax* is increased. A summary for the parameter selection process is shown in Table 7.

Parameter	**w/out cluster reduction**	**w/ cluster reduction**
nbots	≥ 80	< 20
tmax	≥ 300	≥ 100
waitfactor	≥ 3	≥ 4

Table 7. Best parameter ranges for TCA for 1D functions

When the bot cluster centroids were found with cluster reduction, the response curves for *tmax* (flat) and *waitfactor* (exponential) were similar in shape as without cluster reduction, though the curve asymptotically approached a found rate of 86%. The response curve for *nbots* was different, however. The found rate went **up** as *nbots* decreased so fewer bots was better than more bots, assuming that there at least 5 stopped bots in the search space. It appears that for a small number of bots, that there was a smaller percentage of bots in the clusters (say 13 out of 20 instead of 85 out of 90) and those off-clusters bots moved the cluster centers away from the peaks and led to missed detections.
For the final results we used the parameter values *tmax* = 500, *waitfactor* = 4, and *nbots* = 60. We used the same parameter values for all test cases: two different functions (F3 and F4) and with and without cluster reduction. There was a slight dilemma on the choice for *nbots* since more bots did better without cluster reduction and fewer bots did better without cluster reduction so we compromised on 60. We ran the 1D simulations 500 times and the results are shown in Table 8.

	F3				F4			
	Avg # peaks found	Std dev	Found rate	Success rate	Avg # peaks found	Std dev	Found rate	Success rate
w/out cluster reduction	4.052	.9311	81.04 %	97.2%	4.016	.9195	80.32%	97.6%
w/ cluster reduction	4.130	.7761	82.6%	98.2%	4.098	.7782	81.96%	99.0%

Table 8. Final results showing average number of peaks found (out of 5 peaks), found rate and success rate for 500 iterations

The 1D results show that the TCA was very effective at finding a majority of the peaks in the 2 different functions. The success rate was above 97% and the found rate was above 80%. These are good results for an algorithm where the individual particles/bots do not have position information and no bot-bot communication is required.
The results shown in Table 8 are very consistent. The TCA algorithm finds 4 out of the 5 peaks and there is little difference in the results between F3 (peaks of equal height) and F4 (peaks have different heights). There is a slight improvement with cluster reduction, that is, when only the stopped bots are used to determine the peak locations.

5.3 Trophallactic Cluster Algorithm 2D results

The results of a typical two dimensional search using the TCA are shown in Figure 10. The first figure shows a plot of the Rastrigin function with the final bot positions superimposed on top of it. The second figure shows the final bot positions and the centroids of nine clusters found by the K-means clustering algorithm (black stars). Note that six of the cluster centroids are close to actual peaks in the Rastrigin function, but only one of the centroids was within the required tolerance and was thus declared a peak (red diamond).

The initial 2D results, like those shown in Figure 10, illustrate the usefulness of cluster reduction. Figure 11 shows the same final bot positions as in Figure 10, except only the clusters with three of more bots are kept. That is, small clusters of two bots and any bots not in a cluster are eliminated. The K-means clustering is performed with this smaller set of bots and the cluster centroids compared to the peak locations.

After cluster reduction, there are four cluster centroids that are within the tolerance radius of the peak instead on only one centroid. Thus, ignoring the still-moving bots after the conclusion of the search clarifies the definition of the clusters of bots. This in turn leads to more accurate identification of the peaks in the function.

As with the 1D test functions, computer simulations were conducted to refine the three parameters of *tmax*, *nbots*, and *waitfactor* for the 2D case. The results from these simulations for *nbots* and *tmax* are shown in Figure 12. Each graph shows the found rate as the parameter was varied; they are the result of averaging 100 simulations for each set of parameters. For found rate vs *nbots* graph, *tmax* was set to 1600 and *waitfactor* was set to 4. For the found rate vs *tmax* graph, *nbots*= 300 and *waitfactor* = 4.

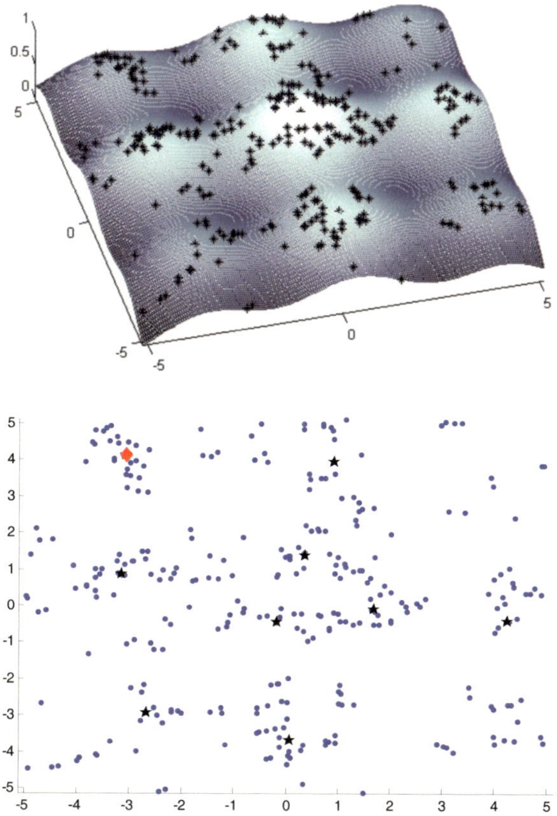

Fig. 10. Typical TCA search results for the Rastrigin 2D function. Left figure: Rastrigin function showing final bot position. Right figure: final bot position with cluster centroids - red diamond denotes found peak and black star denotes cluster centroid.

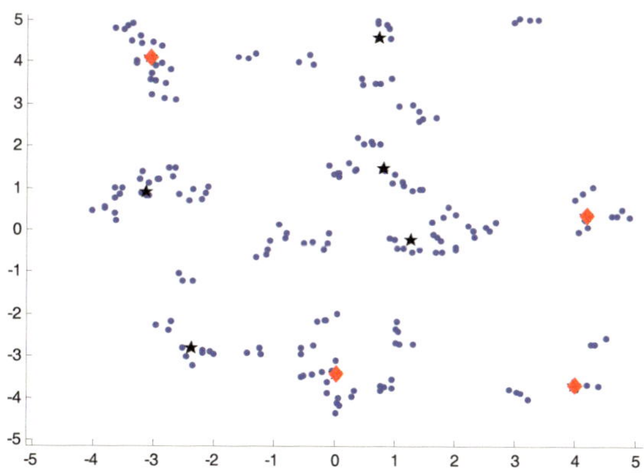

Fig. 11. Analysis of typical TCA search with cluster reduction. Red diamond denotes found peak. Black star denotes inaccurate peak.

The results and interpretation of these two dimensional results are similar to the one dimensional case. The results roughly follow a $(1-e^{x})$ form. Therefore, the appropriate parameter values are again ranges rather than precise values. The values are given in Table 9.

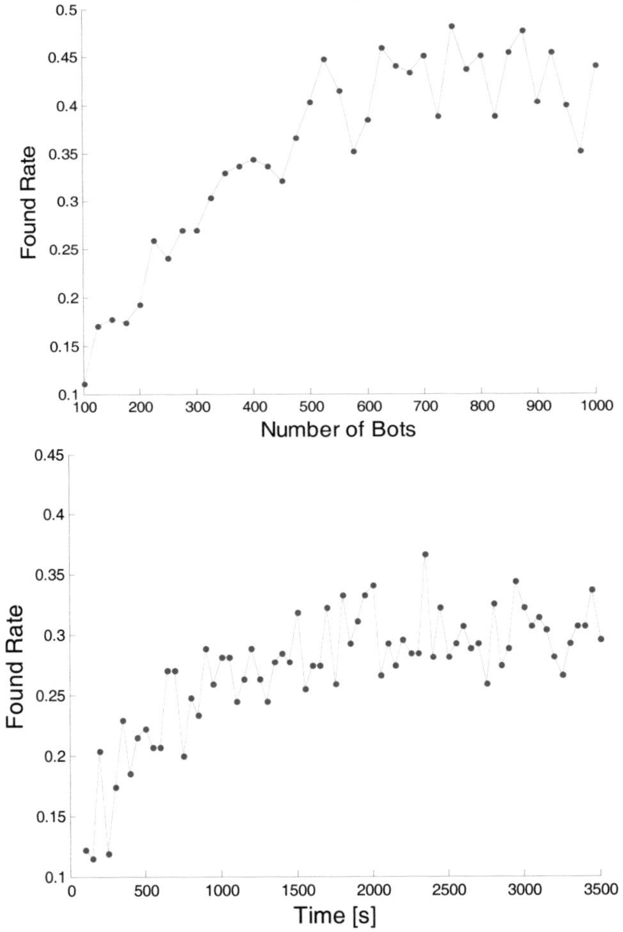

Fig. 12. Results showing found rate vs *nbots* (left figure) and *tmax* (right figure) for Rastrigin function

Parameter	**w/out cluster reduction**	**w/ cluster reduction**
nbots	≥ 500	< 300
tmax	≥ 1600	≥ 1700
waitfactor	≥ 4	≥ 4

Table 9. Best parameter ranges for 2D Rastrigin function

The final two dimensional results were obtained using parameter values *tmax = 1600, nbots = 600,* and*waitfactor = 4.* The same parameters were used both with and without cluster reduction. We averaged the results from 500 simulations and the results are shown in Table 10.

	Avg # peaks found	Std deviation	Found rate	Success rate
w/out cluster reduction	3.7360	1.4375	41.5%	29.2%
w/ cluster reduction	3.3820	1.4888	37.6%	21.8%

Table 10. Final results showing average number of peaks found (out of 9 peaks), found rate and success rate for 500 iterations for the Rastrigin 2D function

The results from the 2D Rastrigin function are not as good as the results from the 1D functions. The lower found rate is due primarily to the fact that the Rastrigin function is a hard function – the peaks do not stand out as prominently as the F3 or even the F4 peaks. In addition, the 2D search space is much larger; for the Rastrigin function, we used a scale of -5.1 to +5.12 for both x and y, while the 1D functions are only defined between $0 \leq x \leq 1$. We increased the tolerance for the 2D results to 0.4 and it appeared that many cluster centroids were close to the actual peaks but, unfortunately, not within the tolerance radius.

6. Conclusions

We developed and tested two biologically inspired search strategies for robot swarms. The first search technique, which we call the physically embedded Particle Swarm Optimization (pePSO) algorithm, is based on bird flocking and the PSO. The pePSO is able to find single peaks even in a complex search space such as the Rastrigin function and the Rosenbrock function. We were also the first research team to show that the pePSO could be implemented in an actual suite of robots.

Our experiments with the pePSO led to the development of a robot swarm search strategy that did not require each bot to know its physical location. We based the second search strategy on the biological principle of trophallaxis and called the algorithm Trophallactic Cluster Algorithm (TCA). We have simulated the TCA and gotten good results with multi-peak 1D functions but only fair results with multi-peak 2D functions. The next step to improve TCA performance is to evaluate the clustering algorithm. It appears that many times there is a cluster of bots near a peak but the clustering algorithm does not place the cluster centroid within the tolerance range of the actual peak. A realistic extension is to find the cluster locations via the K-means algorithm and then see if the actual peak falls within the bounds of the entire cluster.

7. References

Akat S., Gazi V., "Particle swarm optimization with dynamic neighborhood topology: three neighborhood strategies and preliminary results," IEEE Swarm Intelligence Symposium, St. Louis, MO, September 2008.

Chang J., Chu S., Roddick J., Pan J., "A parallel particle swarm optimization algorithm with communication strategies", Journal of Information Science and Engineering, vol. 21, pp. 809-818, 2005.

Clerc M., Kennedy J., "The particle swarm – explosion, stability, and convergence in a multi-dimensional complex space", IEEE Transactions on Evolutionary Computation, vol. 6, pp. 58-73, 2002.

Doctor S., Venayagamoorthy G., Gudise V., "Optimal PSO for collective robotic search applications", IEEE Congress on Evolutionary Computation, Portland, OR, pp. 1390 - 1395, June 2004.

Eberhart R., Kennedy J., "A new optimizer using particle swarm theory", Proceedings of the sixth international symposium on micro machine and human science, Japan, pp. 39-43, 1995.

Eberhart R., Shi Y., Special issue on Particle Swarm Optimization, IEEE Transactions on Evolutionary Computation, pp. 201 - 301, June 2004.

Hayes A., Martinoli A., Goodman R., "Comparing distributed exploration strategies with simulated and real autonomous robots", Proc of the 5th International Symposium on Distributed Autonomous Robotic Systems, Knoxville, TN, pp. 261-270, October 2000.

Hayes A., Martinoli A., Goodman R., "Distributed Odor Source Localization", IEEE Sensors, pp. 260-271, June 2002.

Hereford J., "A distributed Particle Swarm Optimization algorithm for swarm robotic applications", 2006 Congress on Evolutionary Computation, Vancouver, BC, pp. 6143 - 6149, July 2006.

Hereford J., Siebold M., Nichols S., "Using the Particle Swarm Optimization algorithm for robotic search applications", Proceedings of the 2007 IEEE Swarm Intelligence Symposium, Honolulu, HI, pp. 53-59, April 2007.

Hereford J., "A distributed Particle Swarm Optimization algorithm for swarm robotic applications", 2006 Congress on Evolutionary Computation, Vancouver, BC, pp. 6143 - 6149, July 2006.

Hereford J., Siebold M., Nichols S., "Using the Particle Swarm Optimization algorithm for robotic search applications", Proceedings of the 2007 IEEE Swarm Intelligence Symposium, Honolulu, HI, pp. 53-59, April 2007.

Hereford J., Siebold M., "Multi-robot search using a physically-embedded Particle Swarm Optimization", *International Journal of Computational Intelligence Research*, March 2008.

Hsiang T-R, Arkin E. M., Bender M. A., Fekete S. P., Mitchell J. S. B., "Algorithms for rapidly dispersing robot swarms in unknown environments", Fifth International Workshop on Algorithmic Foundation of Robotics, December 2002.

Jatmiko W., Sekiyama K., Fukuda T., "A PSO-based mobile sensor network for odor source localization in dynamic environment: theory, simulation and measurement", 2006 Congress on Evolutionary Computation, Vancouver, BC, pp. 3781 - 3788, July 2006.

Jatmiko W., Sekiyama K., Fukuda T., "A PSO-based mobile robot for odor source localization in dynamic advection-diffusion with obstacles environment: theory, simulation and measurement", IEEE Computational Intelligence Magazine, vol. 2, num. 2, pp. 37 - 51, May 2007.

Kennedy J., "Some issues and practices for particle swarms", Proceedings of the 2007 IEEE Swarm Intelligence Symposium, Honolulu, HI, pp. 162 - 169, April 2007.

Morlok R., Gini M., "Dispersing robots in an unknown environment", Distributed Autonomous Robotic Systems 2004, Toulouse, France, June 2004.

Ngo T. D., Schioler H., "Randomized robot trophollaxis", in *Recent Advances in Robot Systems*, A. Lazinica ed., I-Tech Publishing: Austria, 2008.

Parrott D., Li X., "Locating and tracking multiple dynamic optima by a particle swarm model using speciation", *IEEE Transactions on Evolutionary Computation*, vol. 10, pp. 440-458, August 2006.

Pugh J., Martinoli A., "Multi-robot learning with Particle Swarm Optimization", Joint Conference on Autonomous Agents and Multiagent Systems, Hakodate, Japan, May 2006.

Pugh J., Martinoli A., "Inspiring and modeling multi-robot search with Particle Swarm Optimization", Proceedings of the 2007 IEEE Swarm Intelligence Symposium, Honolulu, HI, pp. 332 - 339, April 2007.

Reynolds C. W., "Flocks, Herds, and Schools: A Distributed Behavioral Model", ACM SIGGRAPH '87 Conference Proceedings, Anaheim, CA, pp. 25-34, July 1987.

Schmickl T., Crailsheim K., "Trophallaxis among swarm-robots: A biologically inspired strategy for swarm robots", BioRob 2006: Biomedical Robotics and Biomechatronics, Pisa, Italy, February 2006.

Schmickl T., Crailsheim K., "Trophallaxis within a robotic swarm: bio-inspired communication among robots in a swarm", *Autonomous Robot*, vol. 25, pp. 171-188, August 2008.

Siebold M., Hereford J., "Easily scalable algorithms for dispersing autonomous robots", 2008 IEEE SoutheastCon, Huntsville, AL, April 2008.

Spears D., Kerr W., and Spears W., "Physics-based robot swarms for coverage problems", *The International Journal of Intelligent Control and Systems*, September 2006, pp. 124-140.

Spears W., Hamann J., Maxim P., Kunkel P., Zarzhitsky D., Spears, C. D. and Karlsson, "Where are you?", Proceedings of the SAB Swarm Robotics Workshop, September 2006, Rome, Italy.

Teller S., Chen K., Balakrishnan H., "Pervasive Pose-Aware Applications and Infrastructure", IEEE Computer Graphics and Applications, July/August 2003.

Triannni V., Nolfi S., Dorigo M., "Cooperative hole avoidance in a swarm-bot", Robotics and Autonomous Systems, vol. 54, num. 2, pp. 97-103, 2006.

Valdastri P., Corradi P., Menciassi A., Schmickl T., Crailsheim K., Seyfried J., Dario P., "Micromanipulation, communication and swarm intelligence issues in a swarm microbotic platform", Robotics and Autonomous Systems, vol. 54, pp. 789-804, 2006.

Zarzhitsky D., Spears D., Spears W., "Distributed robotics approach to chemical plume tracing," Proceedings of the IEEE/RSJ International Conference on Intelligent Robots and Systems, pp. 2974-2979, August 2005.

2

A New Hybrid Particle Swarm Optimization Algorithm to the Cyclic Multiple-Part Type Three-Machine Robotic Cell Problem

Isa Nakhai Kamalabadi, Ali Hossein Mirzaei and Saeede Gholami
Department of Industrial Engineering, Faculty of Engineering, Tarbiat Modares University
Tehran, Iran

1. Introduction

Nowadays the level of automation in manufacturing industries has been increased dramatically. Some examples of these automation progresses are in cellular manufacturing and robotic cells. A growing body of evidence suggests that, in a wide variety of industrial settings, material handling within a cell can be accomplished very efficiently by employing robots (see (Asfahl, 1992)). Among the interrelated issues to be considered in using robotic cells are their designs, the scheduling of robot moves, and the sequencing of parts to be produced.

Robotic cell problem in which robot is used as material handling system received considerable attentions. Sethi et al. (1992) proved that in buffer-less single-gripper two-machine robotic cells producing single part-type and having identical robot travel times between adjacent machines and identical load/unload times, a 1-unit cycle provides the minimum per unit cycle time in the class of all solutions, cyclic or otherwise. For three machine case, Crama and van de Klundert (1999), and Brauner and Finke (1999) shown that the best 1-unit cycle is optimal solution for the class of all cyclic solutions. Hall et al. (1997; 1998) considered the computational complexity of the multiple-type parts three-machine robotic cell problem under various robot movement policies. This problem is studied for no-wait robotic cells too. For example Agnetis (2000) found an optimal part schedule for no-wait robotic cells with three and two machines. Agnetis and pacciarelli (2000) have studied partscheduling problem for no-wait robotic cells, and found the complexity of the problem. Crama et al. (2000) studied flow-shop scheduling problems, models for such problems, and complexity of theses problems. Dawande et al. (2005) reviewed the recent developments in robotic cells and, provided a classification scheme for robotic cells scheduling problem. Some other special cases have been studied such as: Drobouchevitch et al. (2006) provided a model for cyclic production in a dual-gripper robotic cell. Gultekin et al. (2006) studied robotic cell scheduling problem with tooling constraints for a two-machine robotic cell where some operations can only be processed on the first machine and some others can only be processed on the second machine and the remaining can be processed on both machines.

Gultekin et al. (2007) considered a flexible manufacturing robotic cell with identical parts in which machines are able to do different operations and the operation time is not system parameter and is variable. They proposed a lower bound for 1-unit cycles and 2-unit cycles. Sriskandarajah et al. (1998) classified the part sequence problems associated with different robot movement policies, in this chapter a robot movement policy is considered, which its part scheduling problem is NP-Hard, and Baghchi et al. (2006) proposed to solve this problem, by a heuristic or meta-heuristic. In this chapter a meta-heuristic method based on particle swarm optimization is applied to solve the problem.
In this chapter an m-machine flexible cyclic cell is considered. All parts in an MPS (A minimal part set) visit each machine in the same order, the production environment is cyclic, and parts are produced at the same order repeatedly.
In this chapter, we consider multiple-type parts three-machine robotic cells which have operational flexibility in which the operations can be performed in any order; moreover each machine can be configured to perform any operation. To explain the problem, consider a machining centre where three machine tools are located and a robot is used to feed the machines namely M_1, M_2, M_3 (see figure 1). All parts are brought to and removed from the robotic cell by Automated Storage & Retrieval System (AS/RS). The pallets and feeders of the AS/RS system allow hundreds of parts to be loaded into the cell without human intervention. The machines can be configured to perform any operation.

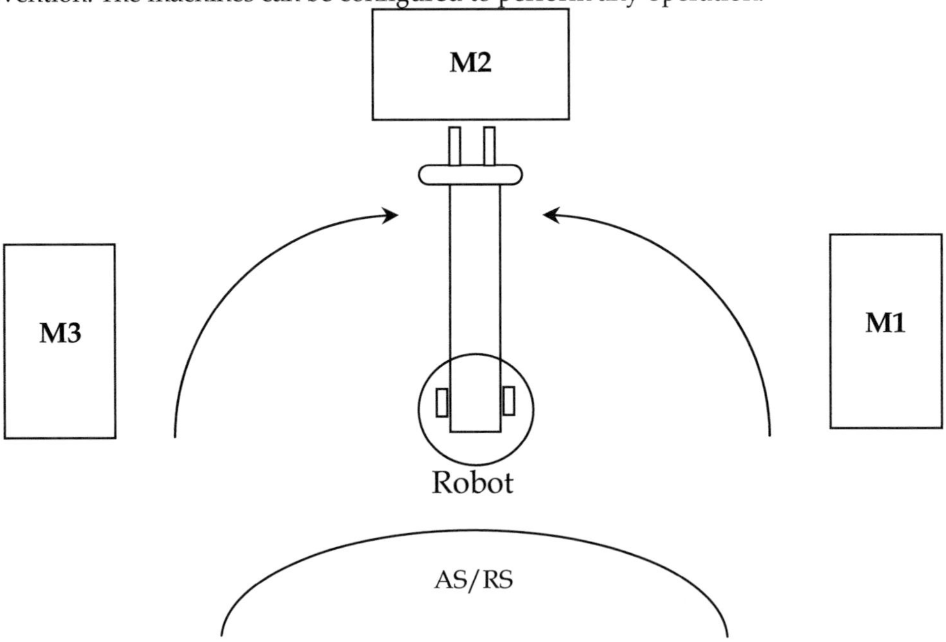

Fig. 1. Robotic work cell layout with three machines

The aim of this chapter is to find a schedule for the robot movement and the sequence of parts to maximize throughput (i.e., to minimize cycle time), as it is showed that this problem is NP-Complete in general (see Hall et al. (1997)). Hence, this chapter proposes a novel hybrid particle swarm optimization (HPSO) algorithm to tackle the problem. To validate the developed model and solution algorithm, various test problems with different sizes is randomly generated and the performance of the HPSO is compared with three benchmark metaheuristics: Genetic Algorithm, PSO-I (basic Particle Swarm Optimization algorithm), and PSO-II (constriction Particle Swarm Optimization algorithm). The rest of this chapter is organized as follows: The problem definition and required notations are presented in Section 2, Section 3 presents the developed mathematical model, and in Section 4, the proposed hybrid particle swarm optimization algorithm is described. The computational results are reported in Section 5, and the conclusions are presented in Section 6.

2. Problem definition

The robotic cell problem is a special case of the cyclic blocking flow-shop, where the jobs might block either the machine or the robot. In a cyclic schedule the same sequences repeat over and over and the state of the cell at the beginning of each cycle is the similar to the next cycle. It is assumed that the discipline for the movements of parts is an ordinary flow-shop discipline. That is a part meets machines M_1, M_2, M_3 consequently.

2.1 Notations

The following notation is used to describe the robotic cell problem:

m : The number of machines

I/O : The automated input-output system for the cell

PT_i : The part-type i to be produced

r_i : The minimal ratio of part i to be produced

MPS : The number of part set consisting r_i parts of type PT_i

n : the total number of parts to be produced in the MPS ($n = r_1 + r_2 + ... + r_k$)

a_i : The processing time of part i on M_1

b_i : The processing time of part i on M_2

c_i : The processing time of part i on M_3

δ : Robot travelling time between two successive machines (I/O is assumed as machine M_0)

ε : The load/unload time of part i

w_i^j : The robot waiting time on M_j to unload part i

S^k : The robot movement policy S under category k

T^k : The cycle time under S^k

In this study the standard classification scheme for scheduling problems: $\psi_1 | \psi_2 | \psi_3$ is used where ψ_1 indicates the scheduling environment, ψ_2 describes the job characteristics and ψ_3 defines the objective function (Dawande et al., 2005). For example

$FRC_3 \mid k \geq 2, S^1 \mid C_t$ denotes the minimization of cycle time for multi-type part problem in a three flow-shop robotic cell, restricted to robot move cycle S^1.

2.2 Three machine robotic flow shop cell $FRC_3 \mid K \geq 2 \mid C_t$

In the three machine robotic flow shop cell, there are six different potentially optimal policies for robot to move the parts between the machines (Bagchi et al., 2006). Sethi et al. (1992) showed that any potentially optimal one-unit robot move cycle in a m machine robotic cell can be described by exactly m+1 following basic activities:

M_i^- : Load a part on M_i $\quad i = 1, 2, ..., m$

M_i^+ : Unload a finished part from M_i $\quad i = 1, 2, ..., m$

In other words, a cycle can be uniquely described by a permutation of the m+1 activity. The following are the available robot move cycles for m=3 flow-shop robotic cell (Sethi et al., 1992):

$$S^1 : \{M_3^+, M_1^-, M_2^-, M_3^-, M_3^+\}$$

$$S^2 : \{M_3^+, M_1^-, M_3^-, M_2^-, M_3^+\}$$

$$S^3 : \{M_3^+, M_3^-, M_1^-, M_2^-, M_3^+\}$$

$$S^4 : \{M_3^+, M_2^-, M_3^-, M_1^-, M_3^+\}$$

$$S^5 : \{M_3^+, M_2^-, M_1^-, M_3^-, M_3^+\}$$

$$S^6 : \{M_3^+, M_3^-, M_2^-, M_1^-, M_3^+\}$$

In this chapter we consider a three machine robotic cell problem under the S^6 policy (Figure 2). The problem of finding the best part sequence using the robot move cycle S^6 is NP-complete (Hall et al., 1998).

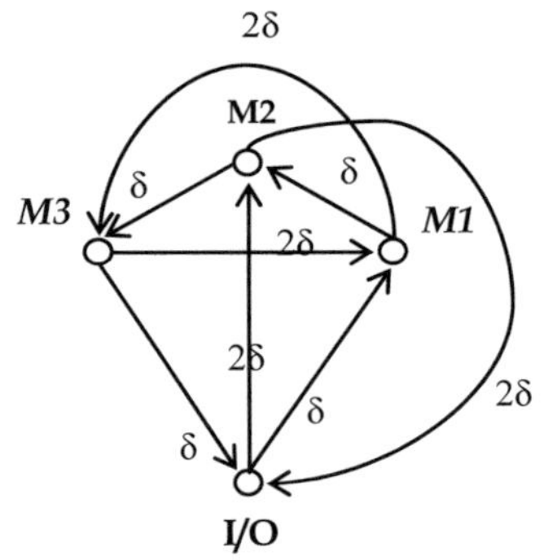

Fig. 2. The robot movement under S^6

Lemma 1. The cycle times of one unit for the policy S^6 are given by:

$$T^6_{I,\sigma(i)\sigma(i+1)\sigma(i+2)} = 12\delta + 8\varepsilon + \max\{0, a_{\sigma(i+2)} - 8\delta - 4\varepsilon, b_{\sigma(i+1)} - 8\delta - 4\varepsilon, c_{\sigma(i)} - 8\delta - 4\varepsilon\}$$

Proof: According to figure 2 the robot movement under policy S^6 is as follow:
Pickup part p_{i+2} from I/O(ε) move it to M_1 (δ) load p_{i+2} onto M_1 (ε) go to M_3 (2δ) if necessary wait at M_3 $(w^i{}_3)$, unload p_i from M_3 (ε) move it to I/O(δ) drop p_i at I/O(ε) go to M_2 (2δ) if necessary wait at M_2 $(w^{i+1}{}_2)$, unload p_{i+1} from M_2 (ε) move it to M_3 (δ), load P_{i+1} onto M_3 (ε) go to M_1 (2δ) if necessary wait at M_1 $(w^{i+2}{}_1)$, unload P_{i+2} from M_1 (ε) move it to M_2 (δ) load P_{i+2} onto M_2 (ε) go to I/O(2δ) then start a new cycle by picking up the part P_{i+3}.
The cycle time by considering waiting times is as follow:

$$T^6_{I,\sigma(i)\sigma(i+1)\sigma(i+2)} = 12\delta + 8\varepsilon + w_1^{i+2} + w_2^{i+1} + w_3^i$$

$$w_1^{i+2} = \max\{0, a_{\sigma(i+2)} - w_2^{i+1} - w_3^i - 8\delta - 4\varepsilon\}$$

$$w_2^{i+1} = \max\{0, b_{\sigma(i+1)} - w_3^i - 8\delta - 4\varepsilon\}$$

$$w_3^i = \max\{0, c_{\sigma(i)} - w_1^{i+2} - 8\delta - 4\varepsilon\}$$

$$T^6_{I,\sigma(i)\sigma(i+1)\sigma(i+2)} = 12\delta + 8\varepsilon + \max\{0, a_{\sigma(i+2)} - 8\delta - 4\varepsilon, b_{\sigma(i+1)} - 8\delta - 4\varepsilon, c_{\sigma(i)} - 8\delta - 4\varepsilon\}$$

3. Developing mathematical model

In this section we develop a systematic method to produce necessary mathematical programming formulation for robotic cells. Therefore first we model single-part type problem through Petri nets, and then extend the model to multiple-part type problem.
A Petri-net is a four-tuple $PN(P,T,A,W)$, where $P = \{p_1, p_2, ..., p_n\}$ is a finite set of places, $T = \{t_1, t_2, ..., t_m\}$ is a finite set of transitions, $A \subseteq (P \times T) \cup (T \times P)$ is a finite set of arcs, and $W : A \to \{1,2,3,...\}$ is a weight function.

Every place has an initial marking $M_0 : P \to \{0,1,2,...\}$. If we assign time to the transitions we call it as Timed Petri net.
The behaviour of many systems can be described by system states and their changes, to simulate the dynamic behaviour of system; marking in a Petri-net is changed according to the following transition (firing) rule: 1) A transition is said to be enabled if each input place *p* of *t* is marked at least with $w(p,t)$ tokens, where $w(p,t)$ is weight of the arc from *p* to *t*. 2) An enabled transition may or may not be fired (depending on whether or not the event takes place). A firing of an enabled transition *t* removes $w(p,t)$ tokens from each input place *p* of *t* and adds $w(p,t)$ tokens to each output place *p* of *t*, where $w(p,t)$ is the weight of the arc from *t* to *p*.

By considering a single-part type system, the robot arm at steady state is located at machine M_2, therefore by coming back to this node we have a complete cycle for the robot arm. The related Petri net for robot movements is shown in Figure 3 and the descriptions of the nodes for this graph with respective execution times would be as follows:

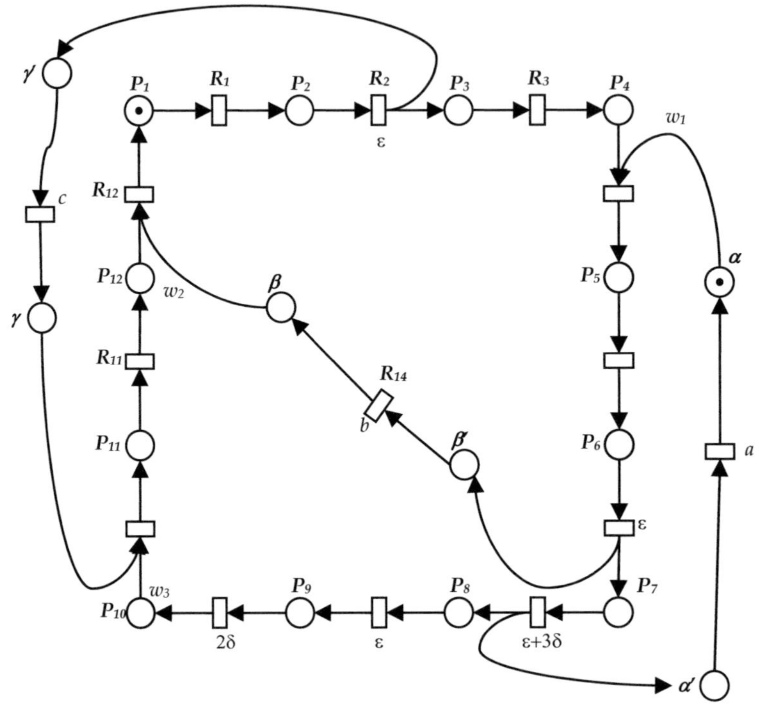

Fig. 3. Petri net for s^6 policy

R_1: go to $M_3(\delta)$; R_2: load $M_3(\varepsilon)$; R_3: go to $M_1(2\delta)$;

R_4: unload $M_1(\varepsilon)$; R_5: go to $M_2(2\delta)$; R_6: load $M_2(\varepsilon)$;

R_7: go to input, pickup a new part, go to $M_1(\varepsilon+3\delta)$; R_8: load $M_1(\varepsilon)$;

R_9: go to $M_3(2\delta)$; R_{10}: unload $M_3(\varepsilon)$;

R_{11}: go to output, drop the part, go to $M_3(\varepsilon+3\delta)$; R_{12}: unload $M_2(\varepsilon)$;

RP_j: wait at $M_j(w_j^i)$ s_i: starting time of R_i; sp_j: starting time of RP_j

α : M_1 is ready to be unloaded;

β : M_2 is ready to be unloaded;

γ : M_3 is ready to be unloaded;

By considering a multiple-part type system, at machine M_1, when we want to load a part on the machine we have to decide which part should be chosen such that the cycle time is minimized. The same thing also can be achieved for M_2 and M_3. Based on the choosing gate definition we simply have three choosing gates as α, β, and γ. Thus we can write the following formulation using 0-1 integer variables $x1_{ij}$, $x2_{ij}$, and $x3_{ij}$ as:

$$\alpha_1 : s_{4,1} - s_{8,n} + C_t \geq \sum_{i=1}^{n} x1_{in}(a_i) + \varepsilon$$

$$\alpha_j : s_{4,j+1} - s_{8,j} \geq \sum_{i=1}^{n} x1_{ij}(a_i) + \varepsilon \qquad j = 2,...,n.$$

$$\beta_j : s_{12,j} - s_{6,j} \geq \sum_{i=1}^{n} x2_{ij}(b_i) + \varepsilon \qquad j = 1,...,n.$$

$$\gamma_j : s_{10,j} - s_{2,j} \geq \sum_{i=1}^{n} x3_{ij}(c_i) + \varepsilon \qquad j = 1,...,n.$$

Definition. A marked graph is a Petri-net such that every place has only one input and only one output.

Theorem 1. For a marked graph which every place has i m tokens (see figure 4), the following relation $s_B \geq s_A + m_i C_t$, where s_A, s_B are starting times of transitions *A* and *B* respectively, and C_t is cycle time, is true.

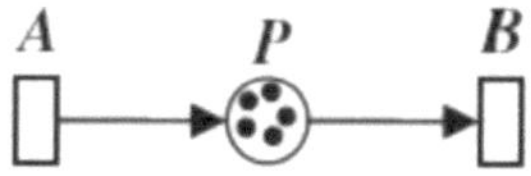

Fig. 4. The marked graph in theorem 1

Proof: see ref. (Maggot, 1984).

In addition the following feasibility constraints assign unique positioning for every job:

$$\sum_{i=1}^{n} x1_{ij} = 1 \quad j = 1,\cdots,n$$

$$\sum_{j=1}^{n} x1_{ij} = 1 \quad i = 1,\cdots,n.$$

To keep the sequence of the parts between the machines in a right order, we have to add the following constraints:

$$x1_{i,j} = x2_{i,j+1} \quad i = 1,...,n, j = 1,\cdots,n$$

$$x2_{i,j} = x3_{i,j+1} \quad i = 1,...,n, j = 1,\cdots,n.$$

Where, we assume that $x1_{i,n+1} = x1_{i,1}$ because of the cyclic repetition of parts.

Thus the complete model for the three machine robotic cell with multiple-part would be as follows:

$$\min C_t^6$$

Subject to:

$$p_{1,1}: s_{2,1} - s_{12,n} + C_t = \varepsilon + \delta \qquad j = 2,\cdots,n \qquad (1)$$

$$p_{1,j}: s_{2j} - s_{12j} = \varepsilon + \delta \qquad j = 1,\cdots,n \qquad (2)$$

$$p_{3,j}: s_{4j} - s_{2j} - w_{1j} = \varepsilon + 2\delta \qquad j = 1,\cdots,n \qquad (3)$$

$$p_{5,j}: s_{6j} - s_{4j} = \varepsilon + \delta \qquad j = 1,\cdots,n \qquad (4)$$

$$p_{7,j}: s_{8j} - s_{6j} = 2\varepsilon + 3\delta \qquad j = 1,\cdots,n \qquad (5)$$

$$p_{9,j}: s_{10j} - s_{8j} - w_{3j} = \varepsilon + 2\delta \qquad j = 1,\cdots,n \qquad (6)$$

$$p_{11,j}: s_{12j} - s_{10j} - w_{2j} = 2\varepsilon + 3\delta \qquad j = 1,\cdots,n \qquad (7)$$

$$\alpha_1: s_{4,1} - s_{7,1} + C_t - \sum_{i=1}^{n} x1_{in}(a_i + \varphi_{a_i}) \geq \varepsilon \qquad (8)$$

$$\alpha_j: s_{4,j} - s_{7,j} - \sum_{i=1}^{n} x1_{ij}(a_i + \varphi_{a_i}) \geq \varepsilon \qquad j = 2,\cdots,n \qquad (9)$$

$$\beta_j: s_{12,j} - s_{6,j} - \sum_{i=1}^{n} x2_{ij}(b_i + \varphi_{b_i}) \geq \varepsilon \qquad j = 1,\cdots,n \qquad (10)$$

$$\gamma_j: s_{10,j} - s_{2,j} - \sum_{i=1}^{n} x3_{ij}(c_i + \varphi_{c_i}) \geq \varepsilon \qquad j = 1,\cdots,n \qquad (11)$$

$$x1_{i,j-1} = x2_{i,j} \qquad i,j = 1,\cdots,n \qquad (12)$$

$$x2_{i,j-1} = x3_{i,j} \qquad i,j = 1,\cdots,n \qquad (13)$$

$$\sum_{i=1}^{n} x1_{ij} = 1 \qquad j = 1,\cdots,n \qquad (14)$$

$$\sum_{j=1}^{n} x1_{ij} = 1 \qquad i = 1,\cdots,n \qquad (15)$$

$$s_{i,j} \geq 0,\, w_{kj} \geq 0,\; x1, x2, x3 \in \{0,1\}$$

4. The proposed hybrid particle swarm optimization (HPSO) algorithm

The particle swarm optimization (PSO) is a population based stochastic optimization technique that was developed by Kennedy and Eberhart in 1995 (Hu et al., 2004). The PSO inspired by social behavior of bird flocking or fish schooling. In PSO, each solution is a bird in the flock and is referred to as a particle. A particle is analogous to a chromosome in GAs (Kennedy and Eberhart, 1995). All particles have fitness values which are evaluated by the fitness function to be optimized, and have velocities which direct the flying of the particles.

The particles fly through the problem space by following the particles with the best solutions so far (Shi and Eberhart, 1998).
The general scheme of the proposed HPSO is presented in Figure 5.

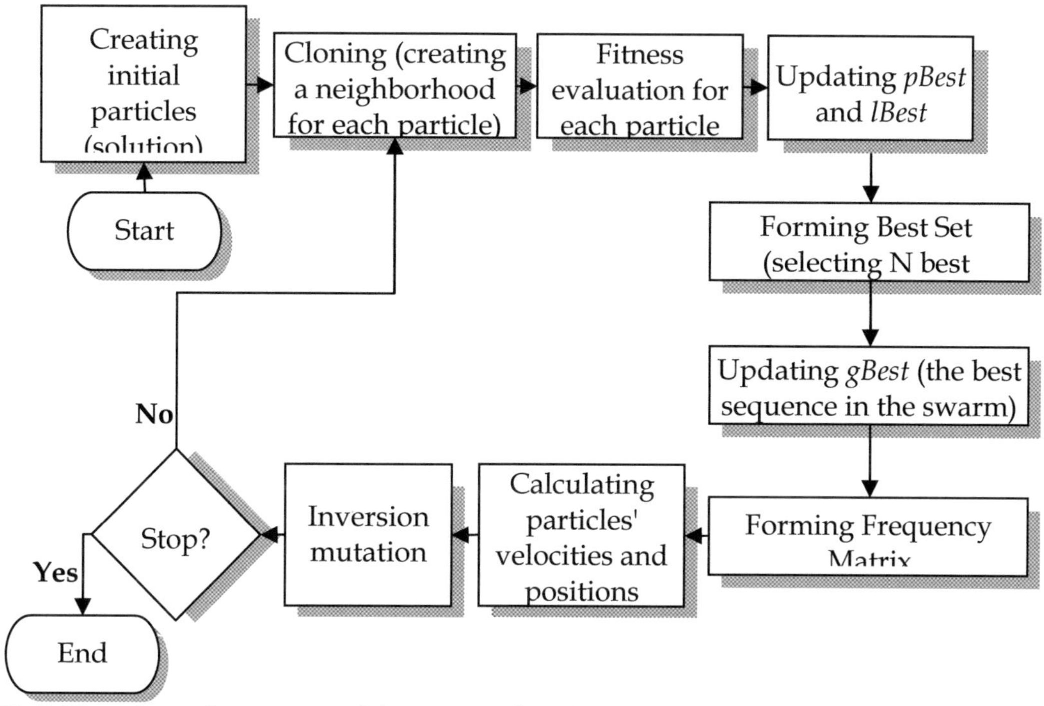

Fig 5. The schematic structure of the proposed HPSO

In this chapter, we extend the discrete PSO of Liao et al. (2007) to solve the robotic cell problem. In the proposed HPSO the velocity of each particle is calculated according to equation (16).

$$V_{id} = wV_{id} + c_1 \times rand() \times (pBest_{id} - x_{id}) + c_2 \times Rand() \times (lBest_{id} - x_{id}) - \left(t/(Number\ of\ Iterations)\right) \times \left(a \times Frequency\ Matrix - b\right) \quad (16)$$

Where c_1 and c_2 are the learning factors that control the influence of *pBest* and *lBest*. w is the inertia weight which controls the exploration and exploitation abilities of algorithm. $rand()$ and $Rand()$ are two independently generated random numbers, t is the current iteration and a and b are two parameters that adjust the influence of the Frequency Matrix on velocity value. *pBest* is the best position which each particle has found since the first step and it represents the experiential knowledge of a particle. After the cloning procedure (the detailed of cloning procedure will be described in the next section), a neighborhood for each particle is achieved. The best particle in this neighborhood is selected as *lBest*.

As Liao et al. (2007), the velocity values transfers from real numbers to the probability of changes by using the equation (17):

$$s(V_{id}) = 1/(1+\exp(-V_{id})) \tag{17}$$

where $s(V_{id})$ stands for the probability of x_{id} taking the value 1. In the proposed algorithm, the new position (sequence) of each particle is constructed based on its probability of changes that calculated by equation (17). Precisely, for calculating the new position of each particle, the algorithm starts with a null sequence and places an unscheduled job *j* in position *k (k = 1, 2, . . . , n)* according to the probability that determined by equation (18):

$$q_i(j,k) = s(V_{id}) / \sum_{j\in F} s(V_{id}) \tag{18}$$

where F is the set of the first f unscheduled jobs as present in the best particle (solution) obtained till current iteration. To achieve a complete sequence, the jobs are added one after another to the partial sequence.
The proposed HPSO terminates after a given number of iterations and the best sequence is reported as the final solution for the problem.

4.1 Cloning

For avoiding local optimal solutions we implement cloning procedure which in summary can be described as follows:

1. *M* copies of the solution are generated so that there are (*M*+1) identical solutions available.
2. Each of the *M* copies are subjected to the swapping mutation.
3. In each clone only the original solution participates in HPSO evolution procedure whereas the other copies of the solution would be discarded.
4. The above procedure is repeated for all of the solutions in the swarm.

4.2 Fitness evaluation

As any metaheuristic algorithm, the HPSO uses a fitness function to quantify the optimality of a particle (sequence). The cycle times of one unit for the policy s^6 are given by:

$$T^6_{I,\sigma(i)\sigma(i+1)\sigma(i+2)} = 12\delta + 8\varepsilon + \max\{0, a_{\sigma(i+2)}\text{-}8\delta\text{-}4\varepsilon, b_{\sigma(i+1)}\text{-}8\delta\text{-}4\varepsilon, c_{\sigma(i)}\text{-}8\delta\text{-}4\varepsilon\}$$

Hence, the following equeation is applied to calculate the fitness function.

4.3 Best Set formation

In the proposed HPSO, to improve efficiency of the algorithm, the best solutions which are obtained so far are selected and kept in the Best Set. Then, the Best Set is applied to forming the Frequency Matrix in next phase of the algorithm.
To form the Best Set, in the first iteration of algorithm and after the cloning phase of the algorithm, the *B* first best particles among all particles in the swarm are selected and placed

in the Best Set. In the other iterations, only the particles that better than the existed particles in the Best Set are replaced with them.

4.4 Frequency Matrix formation

The Frequency Matrix is a matrix which represents the average times that a specific job goes to a specific position according to sequence of particles in the Best Set. To illustrate the Frequency Matrix formation procedure, assume that the following particles are in the Best Set.

First particle (sequence): (1,2,3,4,5)
Second particle (sequence): (1,2,4,3,5)
Third particle (sequence): (1,2,3,5,4)

Therefore, the Best Set will be as follows (Figure 6):

Job \ Position	1	2	3	4	5
1	1	0	0	0	0
2	0	1	0	0	0
3	0	0	.66	.33	0
4	0	0	.33	.33	.33
5	0	0	0	.33	.66

Fig. 6. The example Frequency Matrix

4.5 Inversion mutation

The mutation operator causes a random movement in the search space that result in solution diversity. Inversion mutation is adopted in the proposed algorithm. The inversion mutation, as illustrated in Figure 7, selects two positions within a chromosome at random and then inverts the subsequence between these two positions.

1	8	2	5	4	3	6	7
1	8	3	4	5	2	6	7

Fig. 7. General scheme inversion mutation

5. Experimental Results

The performance of the proposed hybrid particle swarm optimization is compared with three well-known metaheuristic algorithms: GA, PSO-I, and PSO-II. These algorithms have been coded in the Visual Basic 6 and executed on a Pentium 4, 1.7 GHz, and Windows XP using 256 MB of RAM. Note that the performance of the proposed algorithm is also compared with Lingo 8 for small-sized problems.

5.1. Benchmark algorithms

At first, we present a brief discussion about the implementation of benchmark algorithms: GA, PSO-I, and PSO-II.

5.1.1 Genetic algorithm (GA)

Genetic Algorithm (GA) was developed by Holland in 1975 as a tool for solving complex optimization problems of large solution search spaces (Holland, 1992). GAs have been applied successfully to a wide variety of optimization problems to find optimal or near-optimal solutions (Gen and Cheng, 1997). Thus, for evaluating the performance and reliability of the proposed PSO algorithm, we use GA as one of three benchmark algorithms. A pseudocode for the applied GA is provided in Figure 8.

```
Begin;
  Generate random population of N solutions;
  For each solution: calculate fitness;
  For i=1 to number of generations (G);
    For j=1 to N × Crossovr_Rate;
      Select two parents randomly;
      Generate an offspring = crossover (Parent1 and Parent2);
      Calculate the fitness of the offspring;
      If the offspring is better than the worst solution then
        Replace the worst solution by offspring;
      Else generate a new random solution;
    Next;
    Do
      Copy the i^th best solution from previous generation to current generation;
    Until population size (N) is not reached;
    For k=1 to N × Mutation_Rate;
      Select one solution randomly;
      Generate a New_Solution = mutate (Solution);
    Next;
  Next;
End.
```

Fig. 8. Pseudocode for the Genetic Algorithm

5.1.2 PSO-I (Basic algorithm)

In this section, the structure of PSO-I (basic algorithm) is briefly described. The pseudocode of the applied PSO-I is provided in Figure 9.

```
Initialize the particle population randomly
Do
        Calculate fitness values of each particle
        Update pBest if the current fitness value is better than pBest
        Determine nBest for each particle: choose the particle with the best
        fitness value of all the neighbors as the nBest
        For each particle
                Calculate particle velocity according to (19)
                Update particle position according to (20)
While maximum iterations or minimum criteria is not attained
```

Fig. 9. Pseudocode for the PSO-I Algorithm (Shi and Eberhart, 1998)

PSO is initialized with a group of random particles and then search for optima by updating each generation. In each iteration, particles are updated by following two best values. The first one is the location of the best solution a particle has achieved so far which referred it as *pBest*. Another best value is the location of the best solution in all the population has achieved so far. This value is called *gBest* (Shi and Eberhart, 1998). Equation (19) calculates a new velocity for each particle as follows.

$$V_{id} = w \times V_{id} + c_1 \times Rand() \times (pBest_{id} - x_{id}) + c_2 \times rand() \times (nBest_{nd} - x_{id}) \quad (19)$$

Where $Rand()$ and $rand()$ are two random numbers independently generated. c_1 and c_2 are two learning factors, which control the influence of *pBest* and *nBest* on the search process. The global exploration and local exploitation abilities of particle swarm are balanced by using the inertia weight, w. Particles' velocities are bounded to a maximum velocity $V_{\max}$ for managing the global exploration ability of PSO (Shi and Eberhart, 1998). Equation (20) updates each particle's position (x_{id}) in the solution hyperspace.

$$x_{id} = x_{id} + V_{id} \quad (20)$$

5.1.3 PSO-II (Constriction algorithm)

In this section, the structure of PSO-II (constriction algorithm) is expressed in a few words. Also the structure of PSO-II is similar to PSO-I (as illustrated in Figure 4), but in PSO-II the velocity for each particle is calculated according to equation (21) (Engelbrecht, 2005).

$$V_{id} = \chi \left[V_{id} + \phi_1 \left(pBest_{id} - x_{id} \right) + \phi_2 \left(nBest_{nd} - x_{id} \right) \right] \quad (21)$$

Where

$$\chi = \frac{2k}{\left|2-\phi-\sqrt{\phi(\phi-4)}\right|} \tag{22}$$

With

$$\phi = \phi_1 + \phi_2 \tag{23}$$

$$\phi_1 = c_1 \times Rand() \tag{24}$$

$$\phi_2 = c_2 \times rand() \tag{25}$$

Equation (22) is employed by considering the constraints that $\phi \geq 4$ and $k \in [0,1]$. By employing the constriction approach under above mentioned constraints, convergence of the swarm to a stable point is guaranteed. The exploration and exploitation abilities of the algorithm are controlled by the parameter of equation (22): k (Engelbrecht, 2005).

Small-sized problem			Large-sized problem		
No. Of Parts	Problem Number	Problem Condition	No. Of Parts	Problem Number	Problem Condition
5	1	$a_i \geq b_i \geq c_i$	50	22	$a_i \geq b_i \geq c_i$
	2	$a_i \geq c_i \geq b_i$		23	$a_i \geq c_i \geq b_i$
	3	$b_i \geq a_i \geq c_i$		24	$b_i \geq a_i \geq c_i$
	4	$b_i \geq c_i \geq a_i$		25	$b_i \geq c_i \geq a_i$
	5	$c_i \geq a_i \geq b_i$		26	$c_i \geq a_i \geq b_i$
	6	$c_i \geq b_i \geq a_i$		27	$c_i \geq b_i \geq a_i$
	7	Unconditional case		28	Unconditional case
10	8	$a_i \geq b_i \geq c_i$	75	29	$a_i \geq b_i \geq c_i$
	9	$a_i \geq c_i \geq b_i$		30	$a_i \geq c_i \geq b_i$
	10	$b_i \geq a_i \geq c_i$		31	$b_i \geq a_i \geq c_i$
	11	$b_i \geq c_i \geq a_i$		32	$b_i \geq c_i \geq a_i$
	12	$c_i \geq a_i \geq b_i$		33	$c_i \geq a_i \geq b_i$

	13	$c_i \geq b_i \geq a_i$		34	$c_i \geq b_i \geq a_i$
	14	Unconditional case		35	Unconditional case
15	15	$a_i \geq b_i \geq c_i$	100	36	$a_i \geq b_i \geq c_i$
	16	$a_i \geq c_i \geq b_i$		37	$a_i \geq c_i \geq b_i$
	17	$b_i \geq a_i \geq c_i$		38	$b_i \geq a_i \geq c_i$
	18	$b_i \geq c_i \geq a_i$		39	$b_i \geq c_i \geq a_i$
	19	$c_i \geq a_i \geq b_i$		40	$c_i \geq a_i \geq b_i$
	20	$c_i \geq b_i \geq a_i$		41	$c_i \geq b_i \geq a_i$
	21	Unconditional case		42	Unconditional case

Table 1. Problem inctances

5.2 Test Problems

To validate the proposed model and the proposed algorithm, various test problems are examined. The experiments are implemented in two folds: first, for small-sized problems, the other for large-sized ones. For both of these experiments, the values of ε and δ are equal to 1; the processing time for all parts on the all machine are uniformly generated in range [10, 100]. The problem instances are randomly generated as Table 1.

5.3 Parameters selection

For tuning the algorithms, extensive experiments were accomplished with different sets of parameters. In this section, we only summarize the most significant findings:

Genetic algorithm

No of Generation, Population Size, Crossover Rate (Linear order Crossover) and Mutation Rate (Inversion Mutation) for the small-sized problems were set to 50, 50, 1.0, and 0.2, respectively; and for the large-sized problems were set to 100, 100, 1.0 and 0.2, respectively.

PSO-I algorithm

No of Generation, Swarm Size, Learning factors (c_1 and c_2), and V_{max} for the small-sized problems were set to 50, 50, 2, 2, and 3, respectively; and for the large-sized problems were set to 100, 100, 2, 2, and 3. The inertia weight for all problem inctances was set to 1.4 that linearly decreases to 0.9 in each iteration.

PSO-II algorithm

No of Generation, Swarm Size, Learning factors (c_1 and c_2), and V_{max} for the small-sized problems were set to 50, 50, 2, 2, and 3, respectively; and for the large-sized problems were set to 100, 100, 2, 2, and 3. For all problem inctances, k was set to 0.5.

HPSO algorithm

No of Generation, Swarm Size, Learning factors (c_1 and c_2), and V_{max} for the small-sized problems were set to 50, 50, 2, 2, and 5, respectively; and for the large-sized problems were set to 100, 100, 2, 2, and 5, respectively. Mutation Rate, Best Set size, Clone size, and F for all problem inctances were set to 0.1, 7, 5, and 3, respectively. The inertia weight for all problem inctances was set to 1.4 that linearly decreases to 0.9 in each iteration.

5.4 Numerical results

In this section, the proposed HPSO is applied to the test problems, and its performance is compared with above mentioned benchmark algorithms. Each algorithm was executed for 15 times and the mean results were calculated. The numerical results for various test problems are presented in Tables 2 and 3.

Problem no.	Longo 8.0		GA			PSO-I			PSO-II			HPSO		
	OFV[a]	Time	OFV		Time	OFV		Time	OFV		Time	OFV		Time
			Ave.	STD		Ave.	STD		Ave.	STD		Ave.	STD	
1	483	<1	483	0	<1	483	0	<1	483	0	<1	483	0	<1
2	435	<1	435	0	<1	435	0	<1	435	0	<1	435	0	<1
3	363	<1	363	0	<1	363	0	<1	363	0	<1	363	0	<1
4	459	<1	459	0	<1	459	0	<1	459	0	<1	459	0	<1
5	454	<1	458	0	<1	458	0	<1	458	0	<1	458	0	<1
6	404	<1	404	0	<1	404	0	<1	404	0	<1	404	0	<1
7	321	<1	323	0	<1	323	0	<1	323	0	<1	323	0	<1
8	754	1	754	0	<1	754.1	0.3	1	754	0	<1	754	0	1.4
9	763	1	763	0	<1	763	0	1	763	0	<1	763	0	1.4
10	910	<1	910	0	<1	910	0	1	910	0	<1	910	0	1.6
11	825	1	825	0	<1	825	0	1	825	0	<1	825	0	1.4
12	907	<1	907	0	<1	907	0	1	907	0	<1	907	0	1.4
13	753	<1	753	0	<1	753	0	1	753	0	<1	753	0	1.6
14	739	132	741.9	1.9	<1	746.5	6	1	744.4	6.1	<1	741.4	2.4	1.4
15	1312	<1	1312	0	1	1312	0	1	1312	0	<1	1312	0	2.8
16	1272	<1	1272.1	0.3	1	1273.4	1.5	1	1274.2	1.9	<1	1272	0	2.8
17	1212	1	1212	0	1	1212.7	0.6	1	1213.6	1.5	<1	1212	0	2.8
18	1352	<1	1352	0	1	1352	0	1	1352	0	<1	1352	0	2.8
19	1331	<1	1331	0	1	1331	0	1	1331	0	1	1331	0	2.8
20	1222	1	1222	0	1	1226.7	4.4	1	1224	2.5	<1	1222	0	2.8
21	1260	7200[c]	1145.9	18.9	1	1181.5	13.1	1	1178	13.9	<1	1123.6	14.1	2.8

a Objective Function Value
b Standard Deviation
c denotes that the Lingo interrupted after this time and the best achieved value was reported

Table 2. Computational results for small-sized test problems

Problem no.	GA			PSO-I			PSO-II			HPSO		
	OFV		Time	OFV		Time	OFV		Time	OFV		Time
	Ave.	STD		Ave.	STD		Ave.	STD		Ave.	STD	
22	4414	0	12.6	4427.2	4.5	14.5	4424.6	6.0	14.2	4404.6	1.3	98
23	4227.1	0.3	12.2	4239.1	7.8	14.5	4238.4	7.4	14.1	4207	0	98.2
24	3997	0.2	12.5	4026.9	11.3	14.5	4026.8	10.7	14.2	3970.4	4.7	98.6
25	4314	0	13.1	4334.3	6.8	14.5	4332.6	5.2	14.2	4314	0	99.2
26	4283.6	2.3	12.1	4295.1	8.5	14.5	4289.8	3.6	14.2	4257.2	4.8	99.2
27	4360	0	13	4364.3	2.4	14.5	4364.4	2.4	14.1	4360	0	99
28	3405.4	37.1	11.2	3583.1	23.1	14.5	3615.4	26.2	14.2	3385.8	86.1	99
29	6287.8	1.2	19.5	6347	14.6	24.9	6345.4	13.7	24.8	6239.8	20.1	215.4
30	6360.3	0.7	19.3	6437.8	8.7	24.9	6446.2	13.8	24.5	6360.6	1.3	215.2
31	6369.1	0.5	19.9	6469.7	9.6	25.1	6471.4	13.5	24.5	6374.6	12.0	215.2
32	6375.5	0.7	19.5	6431.6	15.1	25.3	6446.4	10.0	24.5	6294.4	37.3	215.2
33	6716.1	1.9	19.3	6764.1	8.6	25	6761.4	7.3	24.8	6701.8	13.4	215.2
34	6357.1	3.9	19.9	6419.4	7.5	25.1	6423.6	10.8	24.8	6329.4	8.2	215.6
35	5843.6	45.1	18.7	6173.3	25	25.1	6181.8	35.4	24.5	5751.6	167.4	215.6
36	8832	0.7	29.5	8889.4	7.6	37.9	8887.8	16.3	37	8812.4	0.9	398.8
37	8693.5	7.3	28.1	8728.5	17	37.8	8747.8	11.8	35.9	8622.6	19.1	398.4
38	8735.9	3.5	27.8	8836.9	20.6	37.8	8842.2	17.0	35.8	8673.2	50.8	400
39	8663.3	2.8	28.7	8861.9	11.5	37.9	8674.6	17.6	36	8585.2	40.1	399.6
40	8125.8	3.9	27.8	8258.3	15.3	37.9	8296.4	11.9	34.3	8111.6	7.8	400.6
41	8588.1	0.3	29.6	8645.7	11.3	38.1	8654	14.6	35.3	8505.0	37.5	398.2
42	7837.9	75.7	27.8	8113.7	30.3	38.1	8163	36.9	36.1	7545.8	97.4	399.2

Table 3. Computational results for large-sized test problems

As shown in Tables 2 and 3, the proposed HPSO is superior to the benchmark algorithms in the most test problems.
As illustrated in Tables 2 and 3, the proposed HPSO consumes more computational time than the benchmark algorithms. Because of the structure of the proposed HPSO, it can search smartly more regions of the search space that results in better solutions. Thus, this higher value of computational time is reasonable.

6. Conclusions

This chapter developed a new mathematical model for a cyclic multiple-part type three-machine robotic cell problem under S^6 robot movement policy that minimizes the cycle time. The developed model is based on Petri nets and provides a new method to calculate cycle times by considering waiting times. It was proved that calculating cycle time under S^6 policy is unary NP-complete. Hence, this chapter proposed a new hybrid particle swarm optimization (HPSO) algorithm to tackle the problem. To validate the developed model and solution algorithm, various test problems with different sizes were randomly generated and the performance of the HPSO was compared with three benchmark metaheuristics: Genetic Algorithm, PSO-I (basic Particle Swarm Optimization algorithm), and PSO-II (constriction Particle Swarm Optimization algorithm). The numerical results showed that the proposed HPSO outperforms the benchmark algorithms in the most problems, especially for large-sized problems.

7. References

Agnetis, A. (2000). "Scheduling No-Wait Robotic Cells with Two and Three Machines." European Journal of Operational Research 123: 303-314.

Agnetis, A. and D. Pacciarelli (2000). "Part Sequencing in Three-Machine No-Wait Robotic Cells." Operations Research Letters 27: 185-192.

Asfahl, C. R. (1992). Robots and Manufacturing Automation. New York, Wiley.

Bagchi, T. P., J. N. D. Gupta and C. Sriskandarajah (2006). "A Review of Tsp Based Approaches for Flow Shop Scheduling." European Journal of Operational Research 169: 816- 854.

Brauner, N. and G. Finke (1999). "On a Conjecture About Robotic Cells: New Simplified Proof for the Threemachine Case." INFOR 37(1): 20-36.

Crama, Y., V. Kats, J. v. d. Klundert and E. Levner (2000). "Cyclic Scheduling in Robotic Flow Shops." Annals of Operations Research: Mathematics of Industrial Systems 96: 97-124.

Crama, y. and v. d. Klundert (1999). "Cyclic Scheduling in 3-Machine Robotic Flow Shops." Journal of Scheduling 2: 35-54.

Dawande, M., H. N. Geismar, S. P. Sethi and C. Sriskandarajah (2005). "Sequencing and Scheduling in Robotic Cells:Recent Developments." Journal of Scheduling 8: 387-426.

Drobouchevitch, I. G., S. P. Sethi and C. Sriskandarajah (2006). "Scheduling Dual Gripper Robotic Cell Oneunit Cycles." European Journal of Operational Research 171: 598-631.

Engelbrecht, A. P. (2005). Fundamentals of Computational Swarm Intelligence. South Africa, John Wiley & Sons, Ltd.

Gen, M. and R. Cheng (1997). Genetic Algorithms and Engineering Design. New York, Wiley.

Gultekin, H., M. S. Akturk and O. E. Karasan (2006). "Cyclic Scheduling of a 2-Machine Robotic Cell with Tooling Constraints." European Journal of Operational Research 174: 777–796.

Gultekin, H., M. S. Akturk and O. E. Karasan (2007). "Scheduling in a Three-Machine Robotic Flexible Manufacturing Cell." Computers & Operations Research 34: 2463 – 2477.

Hall, N. G., H. Kamoun and C. Sriskandarajah (1997). "Scheduling in Robotic Cells: Classification, Two and Three Machine Cells." Operations Research 45: 421-439.

Hall, N. G., H. Kamoun and C. Sriskandarajah (1998). "Scheduling in Robotic Cells: Complexity and Steady State Anhlysis." European Journal of Operational Research 109: 43-65.

Holland, J. H. (1992). Adaptation in Natural and Artificial Systems: An Introductory Analysis with Applications to Biology, Control, and Artificial Intelligence. MA, MIT Press.

Hu, X., Y. Shi and R. Eberhart (2004). Recent Advances in Particle Swarm. Congress on Evolutionary Computation, CEC2004 IEEE.

Kennedy, J. and R. Eberhart (1995). Particle Swarm Optimization. Proceedings of the IEEE international conference on neural networks (Perth, Australia), NJ: IEEE Service Center.

Liao, C.-J., C.-T. Tseng and P. Luarn (2007). "A Discrete Version of Particle Swarm Optimization for Flowshop Scheduling Problems." Computers & Operations Research 34(10): 3099-3111.

Maggot, J. (1984). "Performance Evaluation of Concurrent Systems Using Petri Nets." INFORM PROCESSING LETT 18(1): 7-13.

Sethi, S. P., C. Sriskandarajah, G. Sorger, J. Blazewicz and W. Kubiak (1992). "Sequencing of Parts and Robot Moves in a Robotic Cell." International Journal of Flexible Manufacturing Systems 4: 331-358.

Shi, Y. and R. Eberhart (1998). A Modified Particle Swarm Optimizer. Proceedings of the IEEE international conference on evolutionary computation, Piscataway, NJ: IEEE Press.

Sriskandarajah, C., N. G. Hall, H. Kamoun and H. Wan (1998). "Scheduling Large Robotic Cells without Buffers." Annals of Operations Research: Mathematics of Industrial Systems 76: 287–321.

Comparison of Swarm Optimization and Genetic Algorithm for Mobile Robot Navigation

Petar Ćurković, Bojan Jerbić and Tomislav Stipančić
University of Zagreb, Faculty of Mechanical Engineering and Naval Architecture
Croatia

1. Introduction

Swarm optimization, swarm intelligence and swarm robotics are the fields considering a group of relatively simple individuals able cooperate to perform complex tasks, in decentralized manner. The inspiration is found in the first line within animal societies, such as birds, ants and bees. Social insects exhibit successful behavior in performing complex tasks on the level of the group, and are able to eliminate noise, errors, failure of swarm members. These swarms are robust, able to adapt to constant environmental changes in conditions of limited communications among members and lack of global data. In the context of swarm optimization, the example of Dorigo's "Ant Colony Optimization " (ACO) and Kennedy ad Eberhart "Particle swarm Optimization" (PSO) are most known examples of applying swarm-based concepts to development of optimization algorithms able to cope with hard optimization problems. These algorithms are justifiably called swarm algorithms, because they are run asynchronously and in decentralized manner (Benni, 2004). They also mimic the stigmergic (communication by dynamically changing environment) behavior of swarm of insects.
PSO is inspired by flocking behavior of the birds searching for food. Although PSO shares many common attributes with the field of Genetic Algorithms (GA), such as stochastic nature, population of solution candidates, PSO methods, unlike GA use a kind of cooperation between the particles to drive the search process. PSO methods have no evolutionary operators like crossover and mutation. Each particle keeps track of its own best solution, and the best solution found so far by the swarm. It means that the particles posses own and collective memory, and are able to communicate. The difference between the global best and personal best is used to direct particles in the search space.
ACO employs the search process that is inspired by the collective behavior of trail deposit and follow-up, which is observed within real ant colonies. A colony of simple agents, the ants, communicates indirectly via dynamic modifications of their environment (trails of pheromones) and thus proposes solution to a problem, based their collective experience.
Honey Bees Mating Algorithm (HBMA) can also be observed as a typical swarm based approach to optimization. The algorithm is inspired by behavior of eusocial insects, which are characterized by three main features: cooperation among adults in brood care and nest construction, overlapping of at least two generations, and reproductive division of labour,

respectively. In a recent work, Abbas proposed an optimization algorithm based on honey-bees mating process (Abbas, 2001; Abbas, 2002).
The path planning problem of a mobile robot is to find a safe and efficient path for the robot, given a start location, a goal location and a set of obstacles distributed in a workspace (Latombe, 1991.). The robot can go from the start location to the goal location without colliding with any obstacle along the path. In addition to the fundamental problem, we also try to find a way to optimize the plan, i.e. to minimize the time required or distance travelled (Du et al., 2005; Sadati and Taheri,2002; Ramakrishnan and Zein-Sabatto, 2002).
The popular methods are the visibility graph algorithm and the artificial potential field algorithm. However, the former lacks flexibility and the latter is prone to suffer from difficulties with local minima (Alexopoulos and Griffin, 1992; Chen and Liu, 1997). Neural network and genetic algorithm have been shown to be very efficient in robot navigation (Zarate et al., 2002). General path planning methods based on neural network always establish the neural network model for a robot from the start position to the goal position and entail much computational time. The input data of the model are the previous distance values and position or direction from the sensors. The output data are the next position or direction by self-learning process.
Genetic algorithm is multisearch algorithm based on the principles of natural genetics and natural selection (Goldberg, 1989). Genetic algorithm provides a robust search in complex spaces and is usually computationally less expensive than other search algorithms. Genetic algorithm searches the solution from a population of points and is less likely to be trapped in a local optimum. Many results in the literature show the good application of genetic algorithm in robot path planning (Khoogar and Parker, 1991; Ram et al., 1994).
In this chapter, concept of swarm intelligence, as an optimization technique is proposed for finding collision free paths in work space containing differently shaped and distributed obstacles. Thus, the problem of path planning is considered as an optimization problem, whereat collision free paths receive higher fitness values relative to those resulting in collision with an obstacle. Performance of HBMA algorithm is compared to the performance of a GA developed for the same purpose on two examples, Diophantine equation problem and path planning problem.
Organization of the chapter is as follows: in section 2 we briefly describe colony of Honey Bees, as they are in nature. Section 3 describes proposed abstraction and simplification and describes core elements of the algorithm. In section 4 and 5 HBMA is compared with GA for the first test case, Diophantine equation, and the performances of both algorithms in terms of completeness of the solution and speed of the convergence are discussed. In sections 5 and 6 both algorithms are applied to the second test case, path planning. We conclude with section 7 by finally comparing both algorithms and proposing further possibilities of improving and testing of the described algorithms.

2. Structure of a Honey-Bee Colony

A honey-bee colony typically consists of a single egg laying queen, usually from zero to several thousands drones and 10000 to 60000 workers. Drones are the fathers of the colony. They are haploid and act to amplify their mother's genome without alteration of their genetic composition except through mutation. Workers specialize in brood care and sometimes lay eggs. Broods arise from either fertilized or unfertilized eggs, whereby the former represent potential queens or workers, and the latter represent prospective drones. The mating process occurs during mating-flights far from the nest. A mating flight starts with the dance where the drones follow the queen and mate with her in the air. In a typical mating-flight, each queen mates with seven to twenty drones. In each mating, sperm reaches the sprematheca and accumulates there to form the genetic pool of the colony. Each time a queen lays fertilized eggs, she retrieves at random a mixture of the sperms accumulated in the spermatheca to fertilize the egg.

3. Artificial Model

The main processes of the algorithm are: mating flight of the queen with the drones, creation of new broods by the queen, improvement of the broods by workers, adaptation of workers fitness, replacement of the queen with the fitter brood. The mating flight may be considered as a set of transitions in a state-space (the environment) where the queen moves between the different states in some speed and mates with the drone encountered at each state probabilistically, according to (1).

At the start of the flight, the queen is initialized with some energy content, typically this is a random value from range (0,1] and returns to her nest when energy content equals to zero or when her spermatheca is full. In developing the algorithm, the functionality of workers is restricted to brood care, and therefore, each worker may be represented as a different heuristic which acts to improve a set of broods.

A drone mates with a queen probabilistically according to annealing function:

$$prob(Q,D) = e^{-\frac{\Delta(f)}{S(t)}} \quad (1)$$

Where *prob*(Q,D) represents the probability of successful mating, i.e. the probability of adding drone's D sperm to queen's Q spermatheca. Δ(f) is the absolute difference between the fitness of the drone and the queen, and S(t) is the speed of the queen at time t.

According to defined annealing function, the probability of mating is high when either the queen is the start of her flight, and therefore, her speed is high, or when the fitness of the new potential drone is similar to the queen's fitness. The main steps of the algorithm are presented in Fig. 1.

After each transition in space, the queen's speed S(t) and energy E(t) decay using the following equations:

$$S(t+1) = \alpha \cdot S(t) \quad (2)$$

$$E(t+1) = E(t) - \gamma \quad (3)$$

Where α is a factor in range [0.5, 1] and γ is calculated according to expression:

$$\gamma(t) = \frac{0.5 \cdot E(t)}{M} \quad (4)$$

And M is the size of sphermatheca.

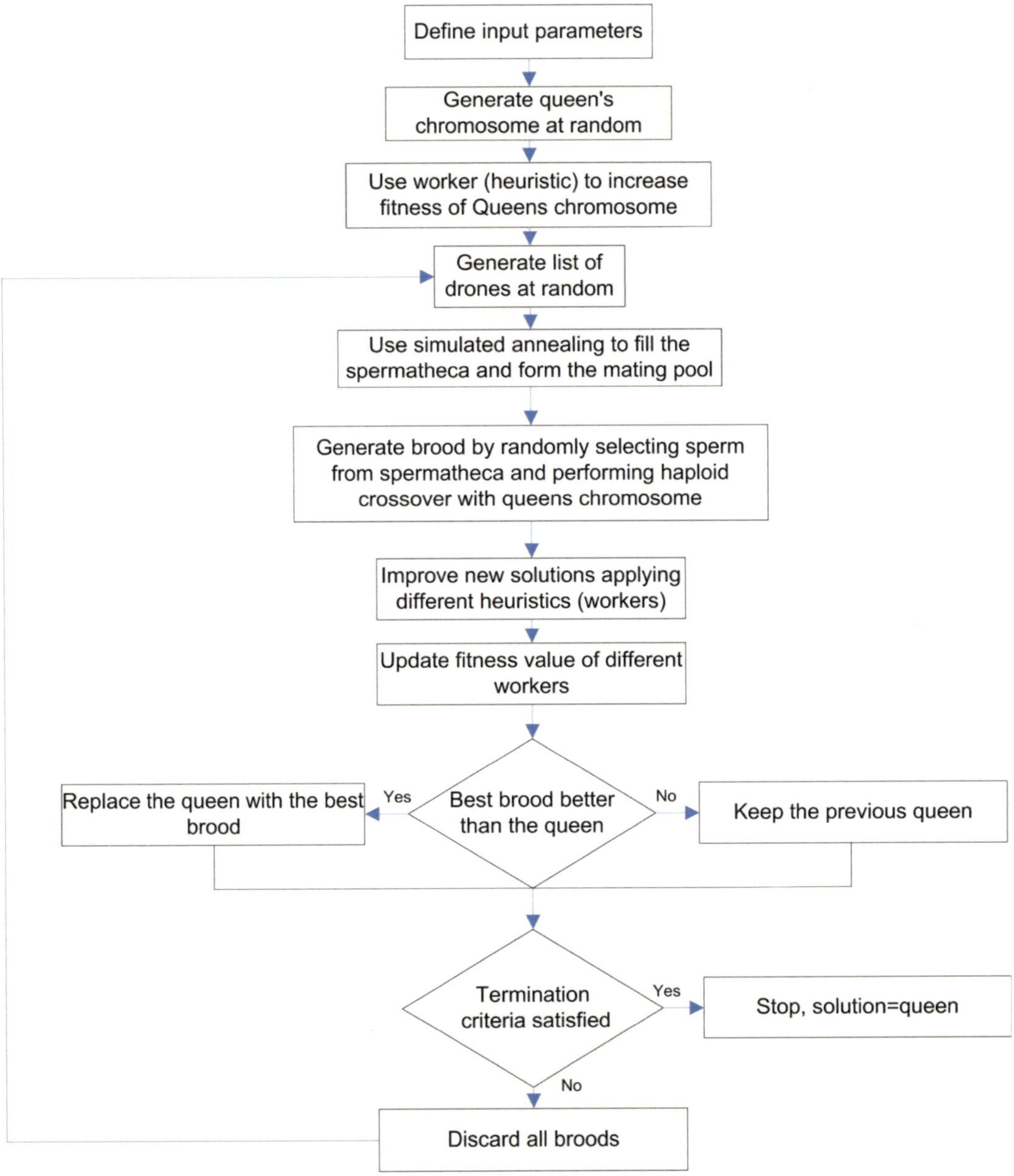

Fig. 1. Flowchart of HBMA algorithm

4. Algorithm Application to Diophantine Equation

In order to perform initial test of the algorithm, we apply the HBMA to a benchmark Diophantine problem. Diophantine equation is an algebraic function (Bull et al., 2006) which must be solved over the integers $x_i \in \mathbb{Z}$. Diophantine problems have a long pedigree in number theory. They also constitute some of the hardest problems in modern mathematics.

Behavior and results of HBMA and GA applied to the Diophantine nonlinear equation, i.e. Markoff equation:

$$x^2 + y^2 + z^2 = 3xyz \tag{5}$$

which has important applications in number theory and known solutions. This example is chosen because it is known how to generate all the solutions in a cube of given size. In the first test case, the problem is reduced to a 2D space by fixing z=433, to have a unique solution, and finding integers that satisfy:

$$x^2 + y^2 + 433^2 - 1299xy = 0 \tag{6}$$

with the search space highly complex in size, as presented with Fig.2.

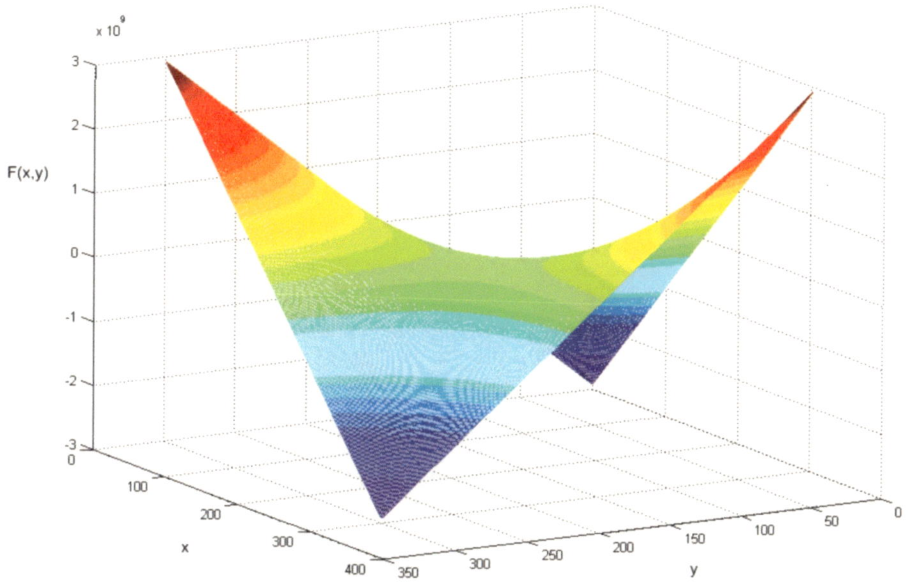

Fig. 2. Search space for the reduced Diophantine problem

5. Results for Diophantine Equation

HBMA and GA were applied to find solutions of the described problem by searching for values in the range $[0, 400]$. Both algorithms were successful finding solutions for the problem, resulting with monotonous shape of the fitness functions, as presented with Fig. 3. and Fig. 4.

The fitness function equals the value defined with eq. (6) and is normalized to the range $[0,1]$. In other words, pairs of numbers which yield lower values of fitness function have higher chances of survival, ideally approaching zero value for solution and termination criteria satisfaction.

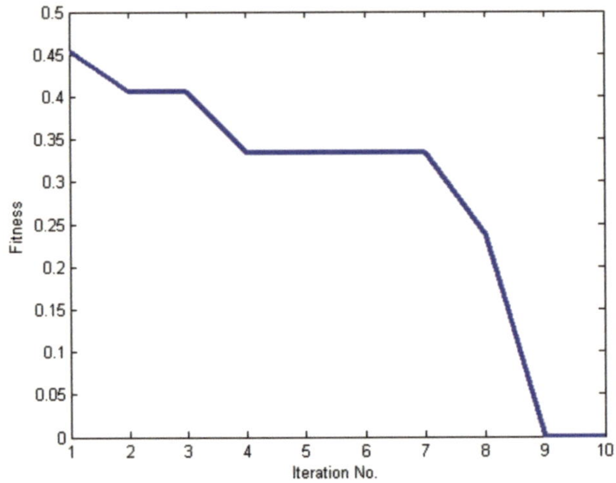

Fig. 3. Fitness value for the HBMA for Diophantine equation

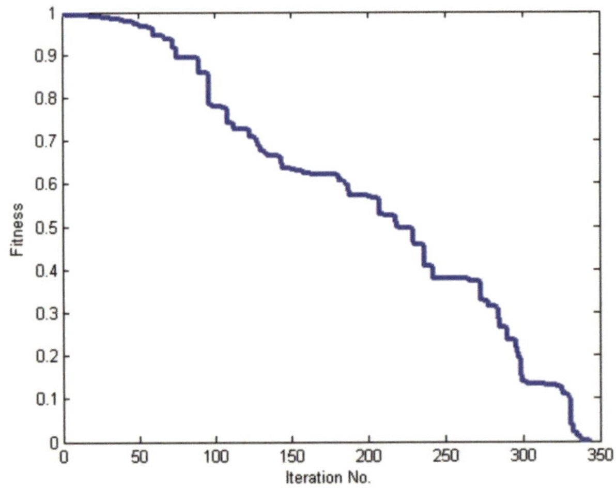

Fig. 4. Fitness value for the GA for Diophantine equation

It is important to notice that performance of the HBMA depend on the *depth of stochastic search*. In this example, only two workers i.e. different heuristics were included; namely, random walk (RW) and two point crossover (2PCO). That means that in each generation of the main loop, a number of local iterations (heuristics) take place for improvement of the brood. In our examples, depth of the local searches is set to 100 iterations.

HBMA has implicitly included elitist function, because the queen is always represented by the best chromosome found so far over all previous generations.
For the GA, 10% elitism is included, meaning that 10% of best chromosomes are directly copied to the new generation, resulting with keeping of best genetic material through the whole evolutionary search. Results and behavior of HBMA and GA are presented with Fig.3. and Fig.4. Fitness values are normalized, and it is possible to directly compare fitness values. In the case of HBMA, the search starts from initial value 0.45, what is likely to be the consequence of the first worker applied to initial queen's chromosome.

	No. of runs	No. of solutions found	Average No of generations	σ_G
GA	30	28	340	44.6
HBMA	30	30	22.9	4.6

Table 1. GA vs. HBMA performance comparison

Both algorithms were tested for 30 runs, with results presented in the Table 1. It could be summarized that HBMA outperforms GA in terms of the completeness of the solution. In terms of speed of the convergence, one should bear in mind that HBMA has inner loop with different heuristics. In each generation, there are number of iterations, defined by the depth of stochastic search, taking place.
Parameters of the GA are: crossover probability: 0.7, mutation probability: 0.01, population size: 30, survival selection: generational, initialization: random, termination condition: solution found or no fitness improvement over the last 50 generations.
Parameters of the HBMA are: sphermatheca size: M=12, stochastic search depth: 100, number of broods: 30, queens energy E and speed S randomly initialized on range $[0.5, 1]$, energy reduction step $\gamma = \frac{0.5 \cdot E(t)}{M}$, heuristics included: random walk and two point crossover. Termination conditions are: solution found or no queens fitness improvement over last 50 generations.

6. Path Planning Results

HBMA algorithm is implemented to solve the problem of navigation of the mobile robot through the space containing arbitrarily distributed obstacles. The environment presentation is based on occupancy grid representation. Occupancy grids represent the world as a two-dimensional array, with each cell having particular value of 1 (if occupied) or 0 (free cell). In our study, obstacles are presented with pairs of nodes connected by mathematically defined lines. This is a more compact way of presenting obstacles which will be shown as very useful for determining collisions with the KBA. It is possible to create different obstacles as lines, or polygons, both convex or concave easily using this compact representation. To be able to treat the mobile robot a point in the environment, a minimum safety distance is added on the nodes producing a safety shadow around the actual obstacles.

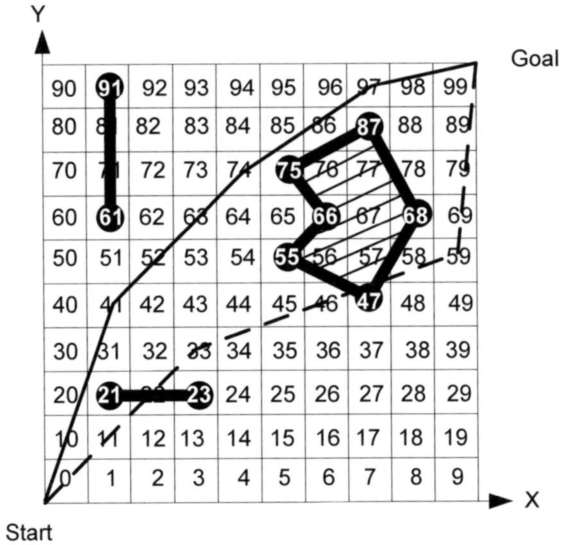

Fig. 5. Environment presented in form of occupancy grid. Numbers denote different nodes. Bold lines: obstacles; solid lines: feasible path; dashed line: unfeasible path.

One possible mobile robot environment is presented in Fig. 2. Obstacles are defined as lines connecting corresponding nodes e.g. nodes 21 and 23 are occupied and connected with the first line, making the intermediate node 22 also occupied. Nodes 55 and 47 are connected with the second line etc. Lines can create different shapes, making nodes falling into the polygons, "unavailable" for the robot. In case of vertical lines, which cannot be defined as mathematical functions since mapping x→y is not uniform, a threshold value is defined such that threshold → 0 and added on the x value of second boundary node of the line. In such manner, line is slightly rotated around the first node, without real impact on the obstacle position and mathematical consistence is preserved.

6.1 Objective Function

Impact of the objective or fitness function has a crucial role on the overall performance of the evolutionary-based algorithms. The main concept in evolutionary robotics has so far been the definition of an effective fitness function (Mermigikis & Petrou, 2006). The authors propose some kind of methodology and state that in order to achieve evolution of useful behaviours, the corresponding fitness function must have the simplest possible form (implicit), it must be possible to be calculated by means of the robot itself (intrinsic) and includes elements of the behaviour itself rather than functional details of how this can be achieved. Proper form and tuning of the parameters can significantly increase speed of the convergence and reduce the possibility of trapping in local optima. In evolutionary-based algorithms, objective function has the role of selection of individuals competing to be selected for the breeding pool and to transfer their genetic material to the new population through the offspring. In the problem being in focus here, the objective function has to reward those individuals (paths) that result in minimal number of collisions with obstacles and travel minimal distance from the start to goal position at the same time. Fitness function is presented by eq. 7:

$$Fitness\_value = \frac{w_1}{A + \sum_{i=1}^{k} a_i} + \frac{w_2}{\sum_{j=1}^{n} d_j} \quad (7)$$

Where w1 and w2 are weight constants, $w_1 \wedge w_2 > 0$, Σa_i is number of collisions of current trajectory with obstacles; Σd_j is total Euclidean distance travelled from origin to destination point for current trajectory composed of n components; A is a constant and $A > 0$.

Fitness function penalizes trajectories resulting with more collisions and larger total distance travelled. To check collisions of the trajectory i and obstacle k, two cases can occur. Case 1: a going-through node falls onto the obstacle. This situation is easy to detect and to handle. Case 2: a part of the trajectory between two consecutive going-through nodes intersects obstacle. This case is handled by solving linear systems of equations for each line segment of the trajectory and for each obstacle as a result of following system of presented with Eq. 8.

$$\mathbf{X} = \mathbf{A}^{-1} \cdot \mathbf{B} \quad (8)$$

Matrices $\mathbf{A}$ and $\mathbf{B}$ contain coefficients derived from lines that describe obstacles and line segments of current path. Matrix $\mathbf{X}$ contains solution of linear system and contains point of intersection of obstacle and linear segment of the trajectory. If intersection point of any line segment S and any obstacle O lies on that particular line segment, then trajectory τ intersects obstacle O. Otherwise obstacle O doesn't intersect trajectory τ.

Formally:

$$\begin{aligned}
&\Theta = \bigcup_{i=1}^{n} O_i \\
&p_i := \left\{ (x, y) | x \in \mathbb{R};\ y - y_< = \frac{y_> - y_<}{x_> - x_<}(x - x_<) \right\} \\
&\lambda_i(y) = \frac{y - y_{<i}}{y_{>i} - y_{<i}} \\
&O_i := \left\{ (x, y) | x \in \mathbb{R}; 0 \le \lambda_i(y) \le 1 \right\} \\
&\tau := \bigcup_{j=1}^{k} S_j \\
&\tau \cap \Theta = \bigcup_{i=1}^{n} \tau \cap O_i \\
&\tau \cap O_i = \bigcup_{j=1}^{k} S_j \cap O_i \\
&S_j \cap p_i = \left\{ x_{ji}, y_{ji} \right\} \\
&\textit{Intersection of segment } S_i \textit{ and obstacle } O_i: \\
&S_j \cap O_i = \begin{cases} \left\{ x_{ji}, y_{ji} \right\} & \textit{for } 0 < \lambda_i(y_{ji}) \le 1 \\ \varnothing & \textit{otherwise} \end{cases}
\end{aligned} \quad (9)$$

Values of weight factors are environment dependent and determined experimentally in this study, although parameterization of environment with regards on number and distribution of the obstacles is considered for future work. This parameterization will include number of obstacles, distribution (spread or clustered) and position of obstacles in environment (along the path connecting initial and goal position, or in corner away of main pathways). Through parameterization, correlation of form of objective function, neural architecture and presented environment could be revealed and thus efficiency of the algorithm further increased.

6.1 Simulation Results

Different environmental setups were used for the experiments. Performance of both algorithms significantly depends on the distribution of the obstacles, namely, whether obstacles are cluttered, concentrated, in the vicinity of the goal position etc. The most difficult environmental setup is when obstacles are cluttered around the proximity of the goal position.

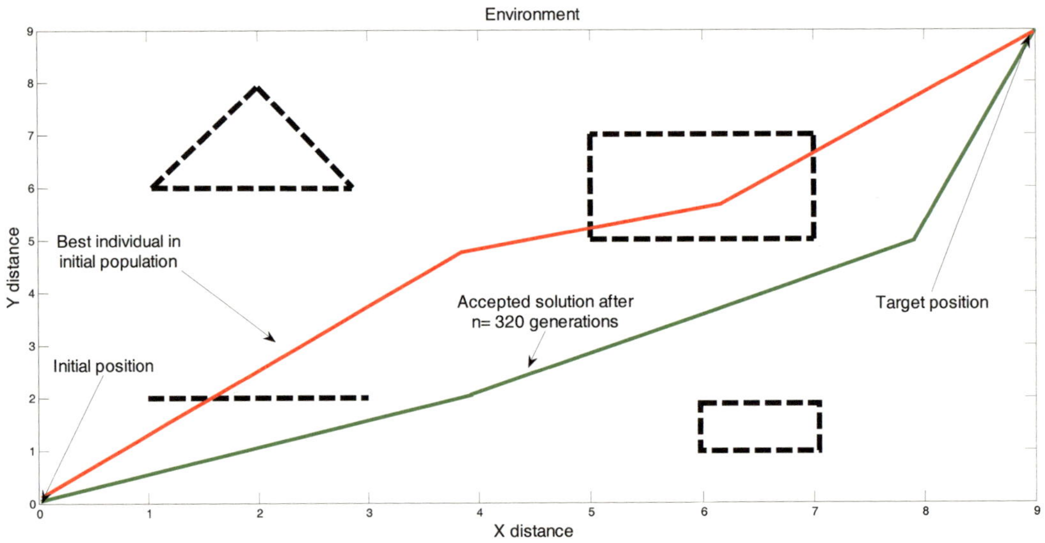

Fig. 6. Environment with obstacles, dashed, unfeasible path, red and feasible path in green colour

One possible environment setup is presented with Fig. 6. Four obstacles are present in the environment with given initial and destination position. For the environment presented with Fig.6., comparison of HBMA and GA is conducted. Results are presented in the Table 2.

	No. of runs	No. of solutions found	Average No of generations	σ_G
GA	500	478	3120	430
HBMA	500	493	430	58

Table 2. GA vs. HBMA performance comparison for path planning problem.

For simplicity, 10 x 10 grid is applied to the environments. Parameters of the GA are: Population size = 50, crossover probability: 0.8, adaptive mutation rate: start with 0.1,

increment 0.1 if no fitness improvement over 50 consecutive steps. Selection is roulette-wheel generational, with the best member of previous generation replacing the worst member of current population. Maximum length of chromosomes (degrees of freedom of trajectory) =15.
Both algorithms are able to find solutions for the presented environment with relatively high confidence. Again is the completeness (total number of the solutions found by the algorithm) slightly on the side of the HBMA. At the same time, number of iterations required is lesser for the HBMA, but CPU time is larger, because of the presence of the internal loop for the brood improvement.
Parameters of the HBMA were the same as in the Diophantine equation example. Regarding the problem of appropriate parameter selection, it is known to be difficult to tune parameters for optimal algorithm behavior, for both algorithms. Parameters were experimentally chosen..

7. Conclusions

HBMA algorithm was developed and compared with performance of the GA algorithm for two test cases. The firs test case was a benchmark Diophantine equation problem. It is shown that HBMA is comparable to the performance of well known GA in terms of CPU time, with the time slightly on the side of the GA. In terms of completeness of the solution, HBMA was able to find all solutions for the given problem, whereas GA twice did not find the solution for given termination criteria.
Similar behavior was observed for the second test case, namely collision free path planning for the mobile robot. However, it is not easy to conclude that HBMA outperforms GA in any way, since both algorithms are stochastic and dependant on the proper selection of parameters. Although both algorithms and objective were designed to be as simple as possible, to enable fair comparison, additional experiments should be performed to achieve more reliable behavior and merits for the algorithms.
HBMA could be further improved by adding additional workers (heuristics) and by monitoring success of different heuristics on different problems. GA could be improved by tailoring specific evolutionary operators for given problems.

8. References

Abass, H.A. (2001). A single queen single worker honey bees approach to 3-SAT, *Proceedings of the Genetic and Evolutionary Computation Conference,* San Francisco, 2001.

Abass, H.A. (2002). Marriage in honey bees' optimization: A haplometrics polygonus swarming approach, *Proceedings of the Congress on Evolutionary Computation,* Seoul, 2001.

Alexopulous, C.; Griffin, P.M. (1992). Path planning for a mobile robot. *IEEE Transactions on Systems, Man and Cybernetics,* Vol.22, No.2, page numbers 318-322.

Beni, G. (2004). From Swarm Intelligence to Swarm Robotics, In: *Swarm Robotics,* Erol Sahin (Ed.), 1-10, Springer LNCS, 3-540-24296-1, Berlin

Bull, P.; Knowles, A.; Tedesco, G. (2006). Diophantine benchmarks for the b-cell algorithm. *In proceedings of International Conference on Artificial Immune Systems* Canterbury, Great Britain

Chen, L.; Liu, D.Y. (1997). An efficient algorithm for finding a collision-free path among poly obstacles. *Journal of Robotics Systems, Vol.7, No.1, page numbers 129-137.*

Du, X.; Chen, H.H.; Gu, W. (2005). Neural network and genetic algorithm based global path planning in a static environment. *Journal of Zheijang University SCIENCE,* Vol.6, No.6, 2005, page numbers 549-554, ISSN 1009-3095

Goldberg, D. E. (1989). *Genetic Algorithms in Search, Optimization, and Machine Learning,* Addison-Weseley, ISBN 02011575675, USA

Khoogar, A.R.; Parker, J.K. (1991). Obstacle Avoidance of Redundant Manipulators Using Genetic Algorithms. *Proceedings of IEEE International Conference on Robotics and Automation,* pp.317-320, Sacramento 1991

Latombe, J.C. (1991). *Robot Motion Planning,* Kluwer Academic Publishers, ISBN 0-7923-9129-2, Boston

Mermigkis, I.; Petrou, L. (2006). Exploring coevolutionary relations by alterations in fitness function: Experiments with simulated robots (2006) *Journal of Intelligent and Robotic Systems: Theory and Applications,* vol.3 No.47 , pp. 257-284.

Ram, A.; Arkin, R.; Boone, G., (1994). Using genetic algorithms to learn reactive control parameters for autonomous robotic navigation. *Adaptive Behavior,* Vol.2., No.2, 1994, page numbers 100-107.

Ramakrishnan, R.; Zein-Sabatto, S. (2002). Multiple Path planning for a Group of Mobile Robots in a 3D Environment Using Genetic Algorithms. *Proceedings of IEEE Southeast Con,*pp.359-363, South Carolina 2002

Sadati, N., Taheri, J. (2002). Genetic Algorithm in Robot Path Planning Problem in Crisp and Fuzzyfied Environments. *Proceedings of IEEE International Conference on Industrial Technology,* pp.175-180, Bangkok 2002

Zarate, L.E.; Becker, M.; Garrido, B.D.M.; Rocha, H.S.C. (2002). An Artificial Neural Network Structure Able toObstacle Avoidance Behavior Used in Mobile Robots. Proceedings of *IEEE 28th Annual Conference of the Industrial Electronics Society,* pp.2457-2461. Spain

4

Key Aspects of PSO-Type Swarm Robotic Search: Signals Fusion and Path Planning

Songdong Xue[1,2], Jianchao Zeng[1] and Jinwei Guo[1]
[1] *Taiyuan University of Science and Technology,* [2] *Lanzhou University of Technology*
China

1. Introduction

Extending the particle swarm optimization (PSO) algorithm to be one of systemic modeling and controlling tools, several research groups investigate target search with swarm robots (simulated or physical) respectively (Doctor et al., 2004; Hereford & Siebold, 2008; Jatmiko et al., 2007; Marques et al., 2006; Pugh & Martinoli, 2007; Xue & Zeng, 2008). The common idea they hold is to map such swarm robotic search to PSO and deal it with by employing the existing bio-inspired approaches to the latter case in a similar way (Xue et al., 2009). Of the mapping relations, some aspects including fitness evaluate and path planning have to be especially considered because PSO-type algorithm working depends heavily upon them. Unlike regarding these respects in PSO, however, the actual characteristics of robot and complexity of sensing to environment make it impossible to be simplified even ignored. Bear that in mind, we might as well explore some representative research work. Pugh et al. compare the similarities and differences in properties between real robot and ideal particle, then extend PSO directly to model multiple robots for studying at an abstract level the effects of changing parameters of the swarm system (Pugh & Martinoli, 2007). Xue et al. simplify characteristics of robot by treating each physical robot as a first order inertial element to study mechanism of limited sensing and local interactions in swarm robotic search (Xue & Zeng, 2008). Doctor et al. discuss applying PSO for multiple robot searches, whose focus is on optimizing the parameters of their algorithm (Doctor et al., 2004). Jatmiko et al. exert mobile robots for plume detection and traversal, with utilizing a modified form of PSO to control the robots and consider how the robots respond to search space changes such as turbulence and wind changes (Jatmiko et al., 2007). Hereford et al. consider how well the PSO-based robot search will scale to large numbers of robots by designing specific communication strategies. Based upon this, they have published results of implementing their PSO variants in actual hardware robot swarms (Hereford & Siebold, 2008). Marques et al. analytically compare PSO-based cooperative search and gradient search as well as biased-random walk search to try to find out which performing well in search efficiency. Due to the exchange of information between neighbors in the first search mode, PSO-type olfactory guided search possesses merit in search properties over its two competitors (Marques et al., 2006).

It is clear that all of works mentioned above neither involve target search with PSO-type control algorithm under conditions of realistic sensing to environment, nor handle the problem of obstacle avoidance in the process of target search. On the contrary, each of them assumes a potential target in search space to give off a diffuse residue that can be detected by a single sensor, which not corresponding with the actual needs and only having theoretical significance (Hereford & Siebold, 2008). In fact, target signals in the real world can not simply be attributed to only one type. Thus, it is need to treat real-time heterogeneous signals fusion rather than measure unisource signals as fitness evaluate. Just take search and rescue in disasters for example. When working miners are confronted with gas outburst accidents in closed roadways, they would be likely to lose touch with outside. Unfortunately, search operations here tend to be difficult because of the extreme risk. Swarm robots may therefore be pitched into carrying out such missions taking the place of human beings. There are multiple kinds of heterogeneous signals, including intermittent sound of call for help and periodic radio frequency (RF) waves as well as continuous gas on disaster spot. We thereupon conduct a case study of target search for propose of PSO-type control. Thus, the rest of this paper proceeds as follows: In Section 2 the system modeling at individual and swarm levels is done to introduce the topics. In Section 3, the properties of target signals are introduced, then a fusion framework is presented. Then, real time path planning strategy for a typical swarm of wheeled mobile robots (WMR) with kinematic constraints in unstructured environment is described in Section 4. To examine the validity of fusion approach and path planning, simulations are conducted in Section 5. Finally, we conclude in Section 6.

2. System Modeling

Consider a swarm of N differentially steered WMRs. The reactive control structure of robot used here makes environment sensing linked with actions directly, without requirement for explicit expression about search space. Meanwhile, the model of our swarm robotic system can be given after mapping PSO to swarm robotic search (Xue & Zeng, 2008). Obviously, the modeling to the system consists of two levels according to abstract degrees, i.e., the microscopic (individual) and the macroscopic (swarm) (Lerman et al., 2005; Martinoli & Easton, 2002; Martinoli et al., 2004).

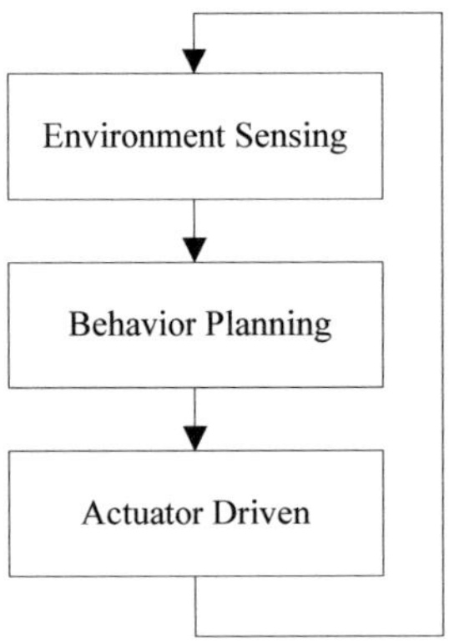

Fig. 1. Control Hiberarchy of Individual Robot

2.1 Modeling for Individual Robot

As the reactive architecture with three functional modules including environment sensing, behavior planning and actuator driven is chosen (Murphy, 2000), see Fig. 1, both proximity sensor system modeling and kinematic modeling should be considered, while the modeling for target signals detection system is dismissed. The reason is that the two former parts are related to path planning and the latter configuration depends on the specific types of target signals rather than physical size of robot and its kinematics.

2.1.1 Proximity Sensor Systemic Model

To integrate collision avoidance mechanism, we assume that proximity sensors (infrared or laser) are equipped on each robot (Jatmiko et al., 2007). Without taking the types and properties of proximity sensors into account, we can only extract the commonness according to the principle of range measurement for modeling. As for the specific configuration of proximity sensors in this work, sixteen proximity sensors are assumed to be equipped on each individual robot, surrounding their body in a discrete circular uniform distributional fashion, see Fig. 2 and Tab. 1 for details, where the black ovals stand for proximity sensors and the arrow points the heading.

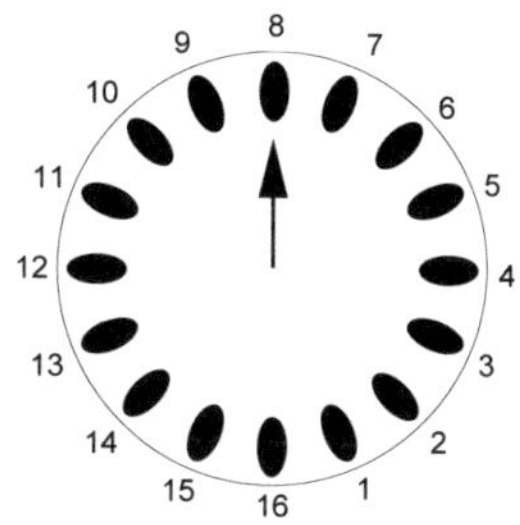

Fig. 2. Proximity Sensor System of Individual Robot

2.1.2 Kinematic Model

The modeling of the kinematics of robots in a two-dimensional plane can be done using either cartesian or polar coordinates. The model in cartesian coordinates is the most widely used and discussion here will be limited to modeling in cartesian coordinates (Maalouf et al., 2006). Typically, the posture of robot at any instant is defined by the position and heading relative to the global frame. The kinematic model is given as follows (Campion et al., 1996):

$$\begin{cases} \dot{x}_i = v_i \cos\theta_i \\ \dot{y}_i = v_i \sin\theta_i \\ \dot{\theta}_i = \omega_i \end{cases} \tag{1}$$

where $p_i = (x_i, y_i)^T$ be position vector or cartesian coordinates of robot R_i under global frame, θ_i its orientation or steering angle, v_i translational or driving or linear velocity and ω_i angular

Sensor Nos.	Degree	Degree	Degree	Degree	Degree	Degree	Degree	Degree
1–8	$-\frac{7}{8}\pi$	$-\frac{3}{4}\pi$	$-\frac{5}{8}\pi$	$-\frac{1}{2}\pi$	$-\frac{3}{8}\pi$	$-\frac{1}{4}\pi$	$-\frac{1}{8}\pi$	0
9–16	$\frac{1}{8}\pi$	$\frac{1}{4}\pi$	$\frac{3}{8}\pi$	$\frac{1}{2}\pi$	$\frac{5}{8}\pi$	$\frac{3}{4}\pi$	$\frac{7}{8}\pi$	π

Table 1. Distribution Degrees of Proximity Sensors

or steering velocity, as is shown in Fig. 3. In the absence of obstacles, the basic motion tasks assigned to a WMR may be reduced to moving between two robot postures and following a given trajectory (Oriolo et al., 2002). Whichever can finally be attributed to the design of control laws, i.e., control command series of inputs $(v, \omega)^T$. Although the actual commands may come in another forms, e.g., the angular velocities ω_R and ω_L of the right and left wheels, respectively, rather than v and ω, we can still make use of analytical module built in robot controller to get the required commands by a one-to-one mapping between these velocities (Oriolo et al., 2002; Siegwart & Nourbakhsh, 2004). For all control schemes, in fact, an additional filtering of original velocity commands is included to account for robot and actuator dynamics.

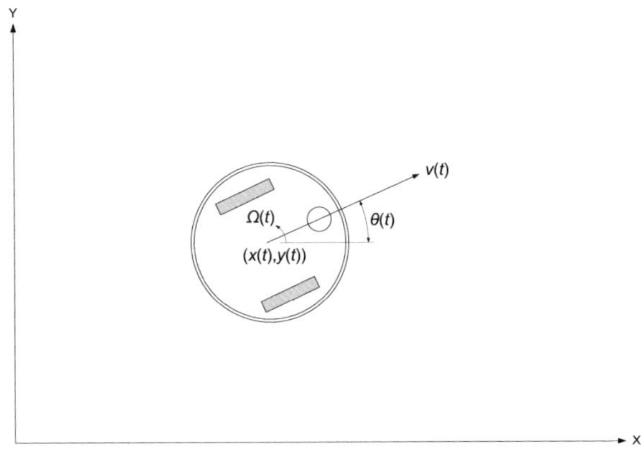

Fig. 3. Kinematic Model of Individual Robot

Due to the abilities of motion mechanism and actuators, there exist limitations on real velocities. Consequently, the actual input commands can be obtained with the following rules:

$$\begin{aligned} v_i &= \begin{cases} v_{max}, & \text{if } v_i(t) > v_{max} \\ 0, & \text{if } v_i(t) < 0 \\ v_i(t), & \text{otherwise} \end{cases} \\ \omega_i &= \begin{cases} \omega_{max}, & \text{if } \omega_i(t) > \omega_{max} \\ -\omega_{max}, & \text{if } \omega_i(t) < -\omega_{max} \\ \omega_i(t), & \text{otherwise} \end{cases} \end{aligned} \tag{2}$$

Note that above rules come from non-holonomic constraints because robot can move along its bearing only, that is, the direction of v_i is always in accordance with the heading of robot, see Fig. 3 and Fig. 4. Then, v_i can be used to decide the orientation of robot R_i. As for the robot at position p_1 with $v_i(t) = (v_{i1}, v_{i2})_t$, we can calculate the orientation:

$$\theta_i(t) = \arctan \frac{v_{i2}(t)}{v_{i1}(t)} \tag{3}$$

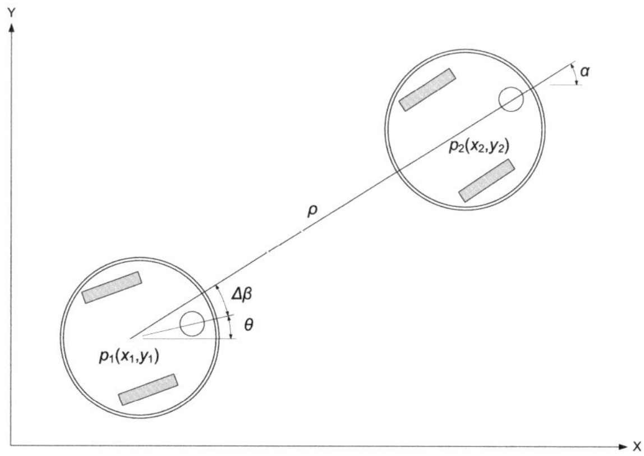

Fig. 4. Motion Control of A WMR

Similarly, the orientation $\theta_i(t+\Delta t) \stackrel{\text{def}}{=} \alpha$ at position p_2 with $v_i(t+\Delta t) = (v_{i1}, v_{i2})_{t+\Delta t}$ can be decided too. Therefore, the required expected turning angle β_i from p_1 to p_2 can be computed and used to further decide ω_i:

$$\Delta\beta_i = \arctan\frac{v_{i2}(t+\Delta t)}{v_{i1}(t+\Delta t)} - \arctan\frac{v_{i2}(t)}{v_{i1}(t)} \tag{4}$$

The posture vectors $(x_i, y_i, \theta_i)^T$ of robot R_i are required as control inputs to individual controller at each time step, depending on the posture estimate with incremental encoder data (odometry). Assume the angular wheel displacements having been measured during the sampling time Δt by the encoders. We can further obtain the linear and angular displacements Δs and $\Delta\theta$. Then, the estimate of posture at time $t+\Delta t$ can be computationally decided (Oriolo et al., 2002; Siegwart & Nourbakhsh, 2004):

$$\begin{pmatrix} \hat{x} \\ \hat{y} \\ \hat{\theta} \end{pmatrix}_{t+\Delta t} = \begin{pmatrix} \hat{x} \\ \hat{y} \\ \hat{\theta} \end{pmatrix}_t + \begin{pmatrix} \Delta s \cos(\hat{\theta} + \frac{\Delta\theta}{2}) \\ \Delta s \sin(\hat{\theta} + \frac{\Delta\theta}{2}) \\ \Delta\theta \end{pmatrix}_t \tag{5}$$

2.2 Modeling for Swarm Robots

Our swarm robotic system is composed of the above-mentioned robots. The meanings of used symbols are as follows: $p_i = (x_{i1}, x_{i2})$ and $v_i = (v_{i1}, v_{i2})$ are position and linear velocity of robot R_i at time t respectively; $p_i^* = (x_{i1}^*, x_{i2}^*)$ and $p_{(i)}^* = (x_{(i)1}^*, x_{(i)2}^*)$ the best historical positions of robot i itself and its communication-based neighborhood (Pugh et al., 2006). Based on this, we can define the best position within its neighborhood (Xue & Zeng, 2008; Xue et al., 2009):

$$p_{(i)}^*(t) = p_k^*(t), \arg_k \max\{I(p_k^*(t)),\ k \in R_i\text{'s neighborhood}\} \tag{6}$$

where $I()$ is the fusion of measurement readings of target signals. Further, we are able to model swarm robotic system with the extended PSO method:

$$\begin{cases} v_{ij}(t+1) = \xi_i v_{ij}(t) + c_1 r_1 (x^*_{ij} - x_{ij}) + c_2 r_2 (x^*_{(i)j} - x_{ij}) \\ v_{ij}(t+\Delta t) = v_{ij}(t) + K_i (v_{ij}(t+1) - v_{ij}(t)) \\ x_{ij}(t+\Delta t) = x_{ij}(t) + v_{ij}(t+\Delta t)\Delta t \end{cases} \tag{7}$$

where $v_{ij}(t)$ and $x_{ij}(t)$ are j-dimensional velocity and position of robot R_i at time t respectively, $v_{ij}(t+1)$ the expected computational velocity, K_i designed parameter of local controller gain which can be chosen by designer. As robot may have to take several time steps $\lambda\Delta t$, in most cases, to reach an expected position from the consecutive previous expected one, adding this factor to obtain a "smoother" displacement. Besides, ξ_i be algorithmic inertia coefficient that can be set constantly or dynamically, c_1 and c_2 cognitive and social acceleration constant respectively, r_1 and r_2 stochastic variables subject to the distribution of $U(0,1)$. We can calculate the linear velocity:

$$v_i(t+\Delta t) = \sqrt{(v_{i1}(t+\Delta t))^2 + (v_{i2}(t+\Delta t))^2} \tag{8}$$

With kinematics model given in Eq. (1), the input of linear velocity (Peng & Akella, 2005) and angular velocity (Siegwart & Nourbakhsh, 2004) can be decided:

$$\begin{cases} v_i(t+\Delta t) = \min(v_{max}, v_i(t+\Delta t)) \\ \omega_i(t+\Delta t) = \begin{cases} \omega_{\max}, & \text{if } \frac{\beta_i}{\Delta t} \geq \omega_{\max} \\ \frac{\beta_i}{\Delta t}, & \text{otherwise} \end{cases} \end{cases} \tag{9}$$

where β_i is the computational expected turning angle from the current position to the next expected one, also see Fig. 4 for details.

3. Signals Fusion

The key to PSO-type search algorithm is to take detection and fusion of target signals as fitness evaluate so as to decide the best-found position, since each individual robot is guided by the best experience of itself own and its neighborhood. Obviously, the temporal and spatial features of different types of signals should be explored in advance.

3.1 Signal Properties

With mathematical models of signals propagation, we can generate a set of theoretically computed signal strength data akin to the empirical data set to design fusion algorithm rather than collect the data on spot.

3.1.1 Sound

The identical model may be used for both propagation and measurement as to the same space. Compared with the size of environment, the mouth of victim can be considered as a point sound source. Let N robots equipped with acoustic sensors construct a mobile sensor field, where an immovable target emits omnidirectional acoustic signals. The signal energy measured on the ith sensor over time interval t, denoted by (Li & Hu, 2003):

$$y_i(t) = g_i \frac{s(t-t_i)}{|r(t-t_i) - r_i|^{\alpha}} + \varepsilon_i(t) \tag{10}$$

where t_i is time delay for sound propagates from target to the ith robot, $s(t)$ is a scalar denoting energy emitted during sampling time t; $r(t)$ coordinates of target during t; r_i coordinates of the ith stationary sensor; g_i gain factor of the ith acoustic sensor; $\alpha(\approx 2)$ energy decay factor, and $\varepsilon_i(t)$ cumulative effects of modeling error of g_i, r_i, α and the additive observation noise of $y_i(t)$, see Fig. 5.

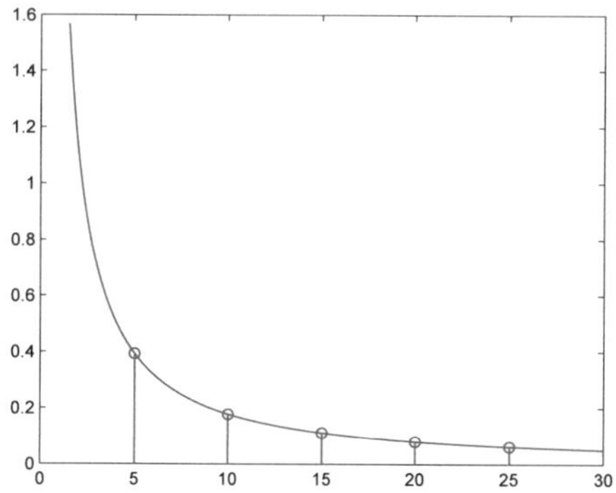

Fig. 5. Acoustic Energy Loss Fitting

3.1.2 RF Waves

Typically, underground mine personnel tracking systems rely more and more upon radio frequency identification (RFID) technologies today. Such a system has basic components including readers and tags. The latter is categorized as either passive or active (Ni et al., 2004). As for coal mine application, a tag is often mounted on a miner's helmet with his lamp. For a radio channel, the transmitted signal reaches receiver via multiple paths (Bahl & Padmanabhan, 2000):

$$P(d) = P(d_0) - 10\alpha \lg \frac{d}{d_0} - \eta \tag{11}$$

where α indicates loss rate, $P(d_0)$ is signal power at reference distance d_0 and d transmitter-receiver distance. The value of $P(d_0)$ can be derived empirically or obtained from the wireless network hardware specifications. In general, η value is derived empirically, see Fig. 6.

3.1.3 Gas

The gas in coal mines will diffuse quickly in closed roadways after gas outburst. The pervasion process can be described as affecting by some odor point sources. For convenience, they can be viewed as only one by linear combination. Let the projection of leak point on the ground be origin, average direction of downwind x-axis, a right hand three-dimensional coordinate system can be set. Then, we can calculate gas concentration in any point on the ground $(z = 0)$ following the law (Marques et al., 2006):

$$C(x,y,t) = \frac{Q}{2\pi\sigma_y(x,t)\sigma_z(x)} \exp\{\frac{(y(t) - y_0(x,t))^2}{-2\sigma_{\bar{y}}^2(x,t)}\} \tag{12}$$

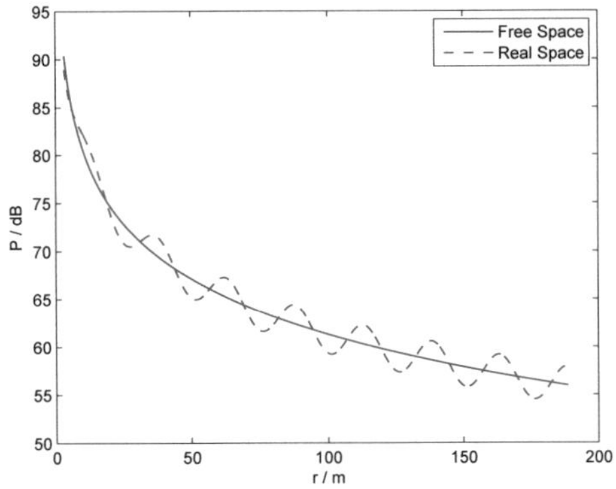

Fig. 6. Log-Normal Signal Loss Distribution

where Q represents release rate, plume center y_0, width w and height h as a function of time t and downwind distance x. $\sigma_y(x,t) = \frac{w(x,t)}{\sqrt{2\pi}}$, $\sigma_z(x) = \frac{h(x)}{\sqrt{2\pi}}$. Fig. 7 shows an example of a time averaged Gaussian plume (Marques et al., 2006). Further, the heterogeneous signals distribution in search environment can be shown in Fig. 8.

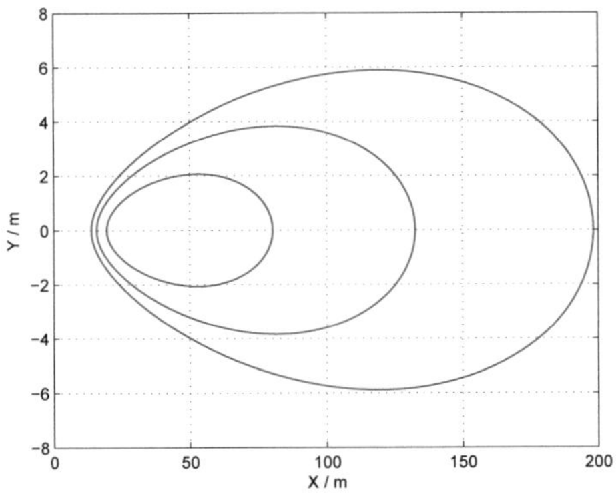

Fig. 7. Gas Concentration Contours on the Ground after Emitted Sufficient Long Time

3.1.4 Signals Propagation Space

The space is divided into six sub-areas (numbered Area 1–6) according to the distribution of signals. The lines in Fig. 8 represent the minimum detectable signal contours corresponding to thresholds $0.0016\,\mathrm{kg/m^3}$, $-90\,\mathrm{dBm}$ and to maximum detectable ranges 200 m, 45 m respectively Li & Hu (2003); Ni et al. (2004). It is need to point out that the sound threshold is not given definitely because it is closely related to the sensor sensitivity. Hence, given a specific power (milliwatt magnitude) of call-for-help in a loud voice, our attention lines in finding how far the emitted sound signals can reach. In simulation, we will make an experiential but reasonable assumption on this value.

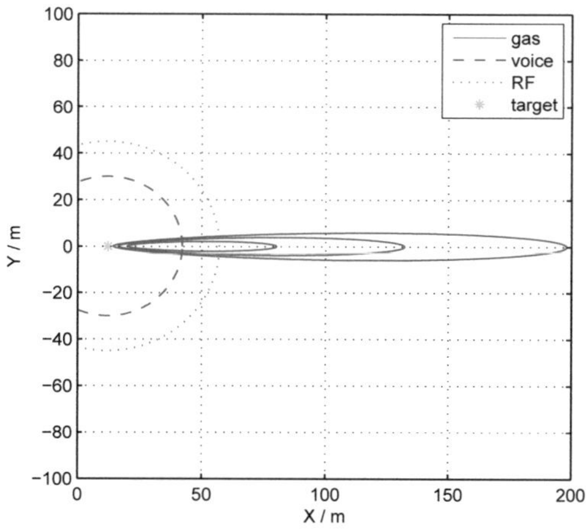

Fig. 8. Signals Distribution in Search Space

3.2 Fusion

Different types of signals are presented in different forms. For instance, gas diffusion distance may be up to several hundreds of meters (Marques et al., 2006); the detectable range of RF waves with frequency $f = 7.5\,\mathrm{s}$ emitted by active tags approach to 150 ft ($\approx 45\,\mathrm{m}$) (Ni et al., 2004) and the localization accuracy with RF RSSI-based method can be 2 m; the detectable range of sound usually reaches not more than 30 m (Li & Hu, 2003), and the estimation error with sound RSSI method may be up to 50%. Therefore, detectable range, statistical properties, localization types and accuracy have to be considered simultaneously in signals fusion.

3.2.1 Sensing Event

Introduce a 2-value logic into describing perceptual process so that we can define perception event in advance. Let A_i ($i = \mathrm{GAS, RF, CALL}$) be perceptual event in event space $\Omega = \{0, 1\}$. Then $A_i = 1$ represents detect-success (beyond threshold) and $A_i = 0$ detect-failure. At the same time, we normalize those measurement readings beyond threshold to $\mathrm{Nm}_i \in (0, 1)$. Clearly, events A_i and A_j ($i \neq j$) are mutually independent and the probability of each event can be calculated with its statistical properties. Further, let $(A_{i\mathrm{GAS}}(t), A_{i\mathrm{RF}}(t), A_{i\mathrm{CALL}}(t))$ be the joint sensing event of robot R_i at time t, then there may be $2^3 = 8$ joint events according to the time characteristic of signals distribution. Again, consider the spatial distribution of signals. Those robots in signal blind area (Area 1) attempt to capture signal clues independently in a spiral move manner to further search for target locally (Hayes, 2002; Marques et al., 2006), without directed by swarm intelligence principle locally, while the robots in Area 2–6 do so (Marques et al., 2006). Thus, it is easy to know that there are six joint events everywhere except source. The possible joint events occurred in each sub-area are listed in Tab. 2. These joint events can be encoded with 3-bit binary numbers. Since the source is characteristic of such encode, we can also express it with 3×1 "characteristic" vector $\vec{C}$. Finally, take the above Nm_is of measurement readings to replace the corresponding elements "1" in vector $\vec{V}$.

3.2.2 Virtual Communication

View signals measurement as continuous communication between robots and target. In this case, each robot possesses its own channel, with source (target) and destination (robot). The individual robot discretizes three types of measurement readings to 1-bit binary digit respectively with corresponding threshold. As for the same signal emitted from source, robots in different sub-areas may obtain different results due to the effect of distance. Consequently, while there are $2^3 = 8$ encodes of full permutation in source, the "received" encodes by robots in different sub-areas may vary. We suppose the duration of emission by target can guarantee the detection success in sampling period (400 ms here). But the transmission time from source to destination is small enough so as to be ignored. Thus, the detection process can transfer continuous information to time- and amplitude-discrete random signal series. Since we suppose Δt be sufficient small interval, the above perception event occurs once at most in every sampling process.

3.2.3 Information Entropy

We can calculate the information entropy from the received information encodes through virtual communication process.

- **Gases.** Robots start to locally search for target as soon as gas can be sensed in global search stage (Marques et al., 2006). As to the continuous gas diffusion, event $A_{\text{GAS}} = 1$ will occur at any time t in Area 2–4 (Hayes, 2002; Marques et al., 2006). Then $P\{A_{\text{GAS}}(t)\} = 1$, i.e., this information is decisive, say, $H(X_{\text{GAS}}) = 0$.
- **RFID Waves.** The perception process of RF signals $\{X_{\text{RF}}(t), t \geq 0\}$ can be viewed as Poisson process with intensity λ_{RF}. As the process has stationary independent increment, those equal intervals may lead to equal probability of $A_{\text{RF}} = 1$. Suppose the sampling period Δt is sufficient small time interval and satisfies the sampling theory. The event $A_{\text{RF}} = 1$ occurs once at most in every sampling. Since events $A_{\text{RF}} = 1$ and $A_{\text{RF}} = 0$ are contrary ones, then we can draw a conclusion $P\{A_{\text{RF}}(t) = 0\} = 1 - P\{A_{\text{RF}}(t) = 1\}$. And the relationship can further be captured by computing probabilities:

$$\begin{cases} P\{A_{\text{RF}}(t) = 1\} = e^{-\lambda_{\text{RF}}\Delta t}\lambda_{\text{RF}}\Delta t \\ P\{A_{\text{RF}}(t) = 0\} = e^{-\lambda_{\text{RF}}\Delta t} \\ e^{\lambda_{\text{RF}}\Delta t} = \lambda_{\text{RF}}\Delta t + 1 \end{cases} \tag{13}$$

"Emitted"	Sub-Area	Possible Event	"Received"
111	1	$(0,0,0)$	000
111	2	$(1,0,0)$	100
111	3	$(1,0,0), (1,1,0)$	100, 101
111	4	$(1,0,0), (1,1,0), (1,0,1), (1,1,1)$	100, 110, 101, 111
111	5	$(0,0,0), (0,1,0)$	000, 010
111	6	$(0,0,0), (0,0,1), (0,1,0), (0,1,1)$	000, 001, 010, 011

Table 2. Joint Event Encodes $(A_{\text{GAS}}, A_{\text{RF}}, A_{\text{CALL}})$ in Search Space

Signal	Entropy	Detectable Range(m)	Localization Type	Accuracy (m)
GAS	0	200	indirect	200
RF	0.0156	45	direct	2
CALL	0.2055	30	direct	15

Table 3. Characteristics of Signals Propagated in Search Space

Accordingly, the entropy of RF signals in information source at t can be calculated with the above conclusion:

$$H(X_{\mathrm{RF}}) = \lambda_{\mathrm{RF}}\Delta t + (e^{-\lambda_{\mathrm{RF}}\Delta t} - 1)\log(\lambda_{\mathrm{RF}}\Delta t) \tag{14}$$

- **Sound of Call-for-Help.** The detected sound of call for help $\{X_{\mathrm{C}}(t), t \geq 0\}$ be Poisson process with intensity λ_{C}. Similarly, we can determine the probability detect-success and detect-failure of call for help to further obtain the entropy of such sound at any time t:

$$H(X_{\mathrm{C}}) = \lambda_{\mathrm{C}}\Delta t + (e^{-\lambda_{\mathrm{C}}\Delta t} - 1)\log(\lambda_{\mathrm{C}}\Delta t) \tag{15}$$

3.2.4 Weight

A criterion to signals fusion can be used by robot. Among all factors, apart from information entropy, the localization type and accuracy with RSSI-based method should also be considered. For instance, gas source is not same as the target location, i.e., we localize target indirectly by localizing gas source based on the fact that one should move quickly upwind in risk avoiding poison gas leakage. Consequently, such estimate may get the worst accuracy (200 m assumed). While the RSSI-based estimate with RF or sound intensity can localize target directly. But the two types of signals differ in accuracy of location estimate, see Tab. 3 for details (Li & Hu, 2003; Marques et al., 2006; Ni et al., 2004). As shown in Eq. (16), the entropy, localization type and accuracy are all required to be integrated by weighted sums.

$$w_i = \frac{aH(X_i)}{\sum\limits_i H(X_i)} + b\kappa + \frac{c}{\tau_i \sum\limits_i \frac{1}{\tau_i}}, \; i = \mathrm{GAS}, \mathrm{RF}, \mathrm{CALL} \tag{16}$$

where logic variable κ represents localization type, "indirect" is assigned 0 and "direct" 1. τ is localization accuracy and $a, b, c \in (0, 1]$ are all positive coefficients that need to be determined empirically. Then, we can take three weight values as elements to construct a 1×3 vector $\vec{W}$.

3.2.5 Signals Fusion

An fusion mechanism for making decision on the best positions is discussed here, being suitable for deciding on cognitive of individual and social of swarm. The mechanism can be expressed with weighted sums operation using vectors $\vec{V}$ and $\vec{W}$, i.e., obtaining the fusion by calculating the inner product of two vectors $fusion = \vec{V}_{(1\times 3)} \cdot \vec{W}_{(3\times 1)}$.

3.2.6 Description of Fusion Algorithm

A full-distributed fusion algorithm run on each individual robot can be presented. First, we assume each robot has an unique ID, carrying a set of sensors and a on-board fusion module so as to measure signals and fuse them independently. Besides, all sensors are assumed to react to signals in sufficient short time. Finally, we design a character structure denoting as "ID"+"Position"+"*fusion*", which can be viewed as the communication protocol. As for the local communication hardware, it can be achieved by wireless transmission systems, like RF or infrared.

Algorithm 1 Real-Time Heterogeneous Signals Fusion

Input: sensor readings
Output: the best-found position and fusion of signals
confirm ID and current position $iPos$;
initialize
    set counter $t \leftarrow 0$;
    set $(A_{i\text{GAS}}, A_{i\text{RF}}, A_{i\text{CALL}})_{t=0} = 000$;
    set $fusion = 0$;
    construct "ID"+"Position"+"*fusion*";{communication protocol}
    set best position of itself $ibPos \leftarrow iPos$;
    set best position of neighborhood $sbPos \leftarrow iPos$;
repeat
    make measurement;
    discretize to 0 or 1 by comparing threshold value;
    format data with characteristic structure;
    if $(A_{i\text{GAS}}, A_{i\text{RF}}, A_{i\text{CALL}})_t = 000$ **then**
        keep silence;{do nothing}
    else
        elect $ibPos$ and update;
        broadcast data within its neighborhood;
    end if
    listen for others;
    if receive data containing $(A_{j\text{GAS}}, A_{j\text{RF}}, A_{j\text{CALL}}) \neq 000$ **then**
        elect $sbPos$ and update;
    end if
    $t \leftarrow t + 1$;
until termination condition is met

4. Path Planning

In PSO-type swarm robotic search algorithm, each individual robot makes decision on its expected destination at every time step as its current target to move towards in a full distributed fashion by combining its own inertia and cognitive experience as well as experience of swarm. The experience of robot itself and its neighbors depends on fitness evaluate, i.e., target signals measurement and fusion, which is discussed in the above section. In other words, the trajectory of each robot "searching" for target is formed by linking a series of expected positions orderly.

Similar to single autonomous robot, path planning of individual robots in swarm robotic system also involves how to move towards their own goals with static/dynamic obstacle avoidance (Warren, 1990). Performed in an iterative manner, artificial potential field (APF) method is usually employed for such task in controlling autonomous robot (Khatib, 1986). Theoretically, robot moves in the direction of the resultant of the attraction force pulling the robot towards the goal, and the repulsive force pushing the robot away from the obstacles. As expected, the robot stops moving after reaching the goal position. Unfortunately, it always suffers from local minima where if trapped (Zou & Zhu, 2003). Looking for a local-minimum-free solution has become a central concern in this approach. Aiming at the problem solving, some modified APF methods are proposed to overcome local minimum. The key ideas may be fallen into two categories: one establishes new potential functions with a few or even no local minima (Ge & Cui, 2000; Warren, 1990); the other uses some techniques to escape from local minima, including random walk (Janabi-Sharifi & Vinke, 1993), wall following (Borenstein & Koren, 1989), and other heuristic methods (Singh et al., 1996). Except for these efforts, Jugh et al. apply the PSO algorithm to path optimization of multiple robots (Pugh & Martinoli, 2006). However, above methods are incompatible with the case of swarm robotic search. New difficulties arise when we apply APF method to swarm robots path planning. One major challenge is to bridge the high-level task planning and the low-level path planning and integrate them into one framework (Ren, 2005). Thus we combine APF method and PSO to plan path towards target with collision avoidance because of low computational cost and better real-time performance.

4.1 Traditional APF

The nature of APF method lines in defining the motion space for robot as a virtual potential filed $U(x)$ including virtual gravitational field $U_G(x)$ and repulsion field $U_R(x)$, in which robot is attracted by target and repelled by obstacles. Then, the resultant force field can be defined with (Khatib, 1986):

$$U(x) = U_G(x) + U_R(x) \tag{17}$$

Meanwhile, we can further define attractive force $F_G(x)$ and repulsive force $F_R(x)$ as the negative gradient of the virtual gravitational field and repulsion field respectively. Therefore, the virtual force $F(x)$ acted by the virtual potential field can be derived using space dynamics equation and Lagrange equation:

$$\begin{cases} F(x) = F_G(x) + F_R(x) \\ F_G(x) = -\nabla(U_G(x)) \\ F_R(x) = -\nabla(U_R(x)) \end{cases} \tag{18}$$

Clearly, the direction of robot motion depends upon the direction of $F(x)$ (Khatib, 1986). Although the traditional APF method has the virtue of being the easiest to implement, it has some limitations above yet. At first, the traditional APF method is applied to the case of global environment information being known rather than the case of environment being partly known or even unknown because the virtual potential field is computationally obtained and what robot sensing environment with its own equipped sensors is not supported. Second, the inherent disadvantage of traditional APF method comes through in being easily trapped to local minima and in target being not able to reach. It is important that the traditional method has to be modified in accordance with robot sensing environment with its sensors. The robot navigates in search space without obstacle collision depends completely upon equipped sensors through collecting measurement readings to judge states including obstacles distribution and possible target position.

4.2 Sensor-Based APF

Generally, when searching for target in unknown environment, the environment map is partly known or even unknown. In this case, the robot behaviors for obstacle avoidance have to rely on continuous local path planning by means of locally sensing surroundings with equipped sensors. As robot moves within search space, the obstacles surrounding robot are inevitably in different conditions. Learning from the traditional APF method to improve real-time property, we can integrate it with the multi-sensor structure of robot to construct virtual potential force with change of sensor readings. Hence, it is need to make some modifications to Eq. (18) based on above structural sensor model, see Fig. 2.

$$\begin{cases} F_i'(x) = F_{iG}'(x) + F_{iO}'(x) \\ F_{iG}'(x) = x_i' - x_i \\ F_{iO}'(x) = \sum_{j=1}^{16} \overrightarrow{\Delta S_{ij}} \\ \Delta S_{ij} = S_R - S_{ij} \end{cases} \tag{19}$$

where $F_i'(x)$ be the resultant force imposed on robot R_i in constructed virtual potential field, $F_{iG}'(x)$ the force attracted by the expected target position, and $F_{iO}'(x)$ the force repelled by surrounding obstacles. Furthermore, S_R be the maximum detection range of all sensors and S_{ij} the current distance reading of sensor j, $\overrightarrow{\Delta S_{ij}}$ represents the increment of the jth sensor reading. Note that $\overrightarrow{\Delta S_{ij}}$ be a vector because of the directionality of sensors.

4.3 Control System Architecture

To decide input commands $(v_i, \omega_i)^T$ of individual robots every time step, the control architecture including swarm and individual levels should be deterministic. From swarm aspect, the architecture is distributed and the PSO-type algorithm runs on each robot. In individual's eyes, robot has a two-level virtual control architecture, which may refer to (Oriolo et al., 2002) for details. Our designed algorithm is at high-level layer, running with a sampling time of $\Delta t = 100$ ms. While the low-level layer is charge of analyzing and executing the velocity commands from upper level. The outputs of algorithm are the command series $(v_i, \omega_i)^T$ in every time step. As is shown in Eq. (9), $v_i(t + \Delta t)$ and $\omega_i(t + \Delta t)$ are the required control inputs of linear and angular velocity at the next time step respectively. While $v_i(t)$ and $\omega_i(t)$ are the obtained current variables by sampling.

4.4 Description of Control Algorithm

It is shown that the PSO-type algorithm is capable of controlling individual robots to move about in space for target search with obstacle avoidance according to the modified sensor-based APF method. Under the conditions of limited sense and local interaction in unknown environment, a valid navigation algorithm can be designed for target search with collision avoidance. Such idea can be implemented in accordance with the three phases below:

- **Compute the Expected Positions.** In terms of the model of swarm robotic system, i.e., Eq. (7), the respected velocities and positions of each robot at time step t can be computational decided by means of interactions within its own neighborhood.

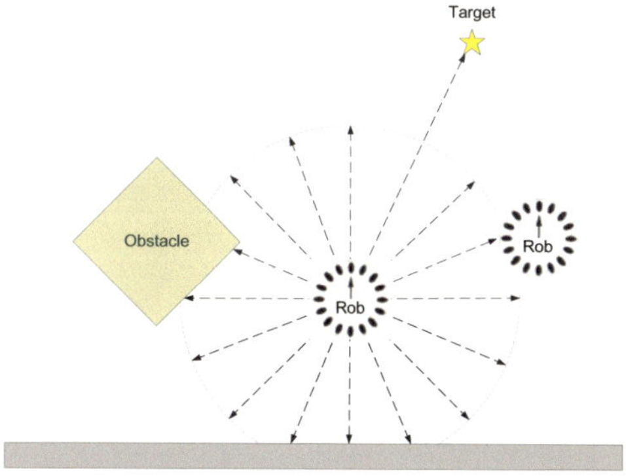

Fig. 9. Schematic of Virtual Force Acted on Robot with Proximity Sensor Readings

- **Decide Virtual Force.** With the modified sensor-based APF model, we can construct a potential field and get the virtual force in this field. The specific way is to take the expected position of robot at time step as the current temporary target which will attract the robot, while the robot will be repelled by the detected static or dynamic obstacles.
- **Compute the Real Positions.** As the velocity of robot at time $t+1$ is gotten, the position of robot at time $t+1$ can be computationally obtained according to the kinematics of robot.

A full distributed PSO-type algorithm for target search is developed, which can be implemented on each robot in parallel. Without loss of generality, we can describe the algorithm run on robot R_i as Algorithm 2.

5. Simulation and Discussions

To elaborate how to fuse the specific heterogeneous signals and how to decide the best positions, the simulations are designed and conducted for the purpose. First, virtual signal generators are arranged where same as target situates, emitting signals following their own time characteristic. Then, a series of detection points are set in signal Area 1–6. Our task is to investigate what happened in each information sink (robot) when different combination of signals is emitted from source by virtually measuring and fusing. We observe for sufficient long time until all eight encodes transmitted from source. Then we try to find the relationship between distance and fusion result.

5.1 Signals Generating

Consider the properties of a given Poisson process with intensity λ. The successive coming time of events obey exponential distribution with mean $\frac{1}{\lambda}$. We can empirically set the value in some interval, for example, the upper bound and lower bound can set to 0.01 and 0.001 respectively, i.e., $\lambda_C \in (0.001, 0.01)$, while the intensity of RF signals can be $\lambda_{RF} = 0.1333$ according to its primitive definition, which reflect the temporal characteristics of target signals.

Algorithm 2 Path Planning for Swarm Robots in A Full-Distributed Way

initialize
  set counter $k \leftarrow 0$;
  initialize constants;
  initialize v^i_k, x^i_k;
  initialize position of target;
  initialize robot's own cognition
    make measurement I^i_k;
    $I^i_{\max} \leftarrow I^i_k$;
    $p^i_k \leftarrow x^i_k$;
  initialize shared information
    $I^g_{\max} \leftarrow I^i_k$;
    $p^g_k \leftarrow x^i_k$;
  confirm index of best individual;
repeat
  $k \leftarrow k+1$;
  communicate among neighborhood
    confirm neighborhood;
    for $j = 1$ to $number\_of\_neighbors$ **do**
      compute I^j_k;
      $I^g_{\max} \leftarrow \max(I^i_k, I^j_k)$;
      $p^g_k \leftarrow x^m_k, \arg_m \max\{I(x^m_k),\ m \in (i,j)\}$;
    endfor
  compute expected velocity and position
    $\overline{v^i_{k+1}} \leftarrow w_k v^i_k + c_1 r_1 (p^i_k - x^i_k) + c_2 r_2 (p^g_k - x^i_k)$;
    $\overline{v^i_{k+\Delta k}} \leftarrow v^i_k + K_i(\overline{v^i_{k+1}} - v^i_k)$;
    $x^i_{k+\Delta k} \leftarrow x^i_k + \overline{v^i_{k+\Delta k}} \Delta k$;
    $\xi_k \leftarrow c_3 \xi_k; \{0 < c_3 < 1\}$
  compute velocity with kinematics
    $v^i_{k+\Delta k} \leftarrow \min(v_{\max}, \overline{v^i_{k+\Delta k}})$;
    compute $\omega^i_{k+\Delta k}$;
      if shared information updated by neighbor **then**
        compute next expected position;
      endif
until succeed in search

5.2 Deployment of Measuring Points

We set a series of measuring points, assigning one with each sub-area. Different points are different far away from the source. Note that a pair of points in different areas having the same distance value are arranged to study the relation between fusions at the same time.

5.3 Main Parameter Settings

We simulate signals fusion using parameter configuration $a = 1$, $b = 0.001$, $c = 1$, $\lambda_C = 0.2055$, $\lambda_{RF} = 0.0156$. For convenience, target is fixed to $(0,0)$ all time and the coordinates of six measuring points are $(100,40)$, $(150,0)$, $(40,0)$, $(20,0)$, $(0,35)$, $(0,20)$ orderly. Meanwhile, we focus on if the coverage of all joint events occur in sufficient long time rather than the moments.

5.4 Map Processing

In study on path planning of autonomous robotics, how to represent the working space, i.e., how to model the space is one of the important problems. Based on the difference of sensing to environment, modeling approaches to known or unknown map fall into two ones. Here we model working space for swarm robots with digit image processing technology. The obstacle information relative to each point in search space is expressed with a two-dimensional arrays. Of representative symbols, 0 represents passable point and 1 passless. The Fig. 10 is the example of mapping processing.

(a) Original Map

0	0	0	1	0	0	0	0	0	0
0	0	0	1	0	0	1	1	1	0
0	1	0	1	0	0	0	1	0	0
0	1	0	0	0	0	0	0	0	0
0	1	0	1	0	0	1	0	0	0
0	1	0	1	0	0	1	0	1	0
0	0	0	1	1	1	1	0	1	1
0	0	0	0	0	0	0	0	1	0
1	1	1	1	0	0	1	0	0	0
0	0	0	0	0	0	1	0	0	0

(b) Digitizing

Fig. 10. Working Space for Swarm Robotic Search

5.5 Obstacle Avoidance Planning

Based on the fusion method, we run the swarm robotic search algorithm having a specific function of path planning. The unequal sized swarms ($N = 3, 5, 8, 10$) are used, repeated the algorithm running for ten times respectively. Then, the statistics about total distance and time elapsed in different cases are collected to support our presented method.

5.6 Results and Discussions

Conducting the above simulations repeatedly, we can get the following results. And then we may hold discussions and draw some conclusions.

- The fused values in simulation are shown in Fig. 11, from which robots can "find" out the best positions by simple election operation. It's perceptible that the bigger the fusion value, the nearer the measuring point from target. At the same time, it is observed that as for No. 4 and No. 6 points, the fusion results are the same in cases of $Source = 001, 010, 011$, and different in cases of $Source = 101, 110, 111$ although they are equal to distance of target. We may explain it in this manner: robots searching for target depend on measurements because they do not know the position of target. While the two points are located in different sub-areas, the situation of signals cover is different.

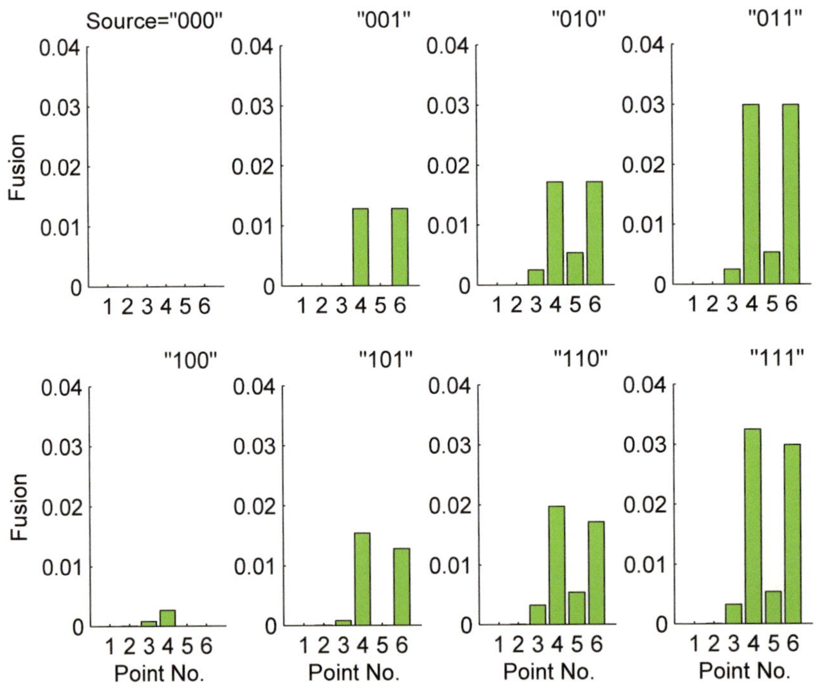

Fig. 11. Fusion results at the assigned six measuring points under different encodes of information source. Note that the title Source="000" of the left corner sub-figure represents no GAS, no RF, and no CALL signals are emitted when sampling. One can understand the other cases in a similar manner. Besides, the fusion is a scalar value without any physical meaning.

- Fig. 12 shows the scenario of two robots decide their respective motion behaviors with modified APF method to plan paths for obstacle avoidance.

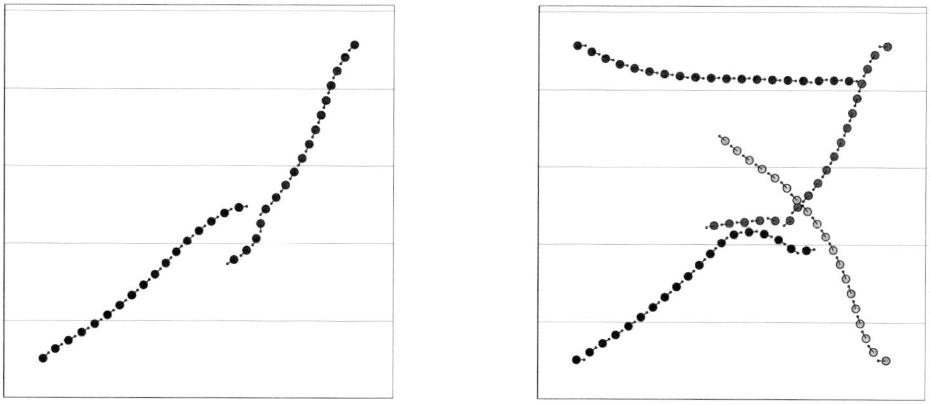

(a) 2-Rob (b) 4-Rob

Fig. 12. Obstacle Avoidance between Unequal Sized Robots with Sensor-Based APF Method

Swarm Size	Average Time	Average Total Distance
3	278	1930
5	232	2410
8	197	3136
10	184	4380

Table 4. Statistics from Search for Target Simulations

- Fig. 13 shows the scenario of one single robot planning its path using multiple sensor-based APF method without obstacle collision to search for target successfully under different conditions of obstacle types.
- Consider the total displacements and time (iterative generations) when the search succeeds. The statistical results shown in Tab. 4 and the relations between average distance/generations and swarm size are charted as Fig. 14.

6. Conclusions

As for PSO-type control of swarm robots, the experience both of individual robots and of population is required. In order to decide the best positions, we take the characteristic information of target, such as intensity or concentration of different signals emitted by target, as the "fitness". Therefore, the problem of multi-source signals fusion is proposed. To this end, we model the process of signals measurement with robot sensors as virtual communication. Then, the detected target signals can be viewed as transmitted encodes with respect to information source. We thereupon present some concepts of binary logic and perceptual event to describe the "communication" between target and robots. Besides, we also put forward information entropy-based fusion criteria and priority to fuse signals and election mechanism

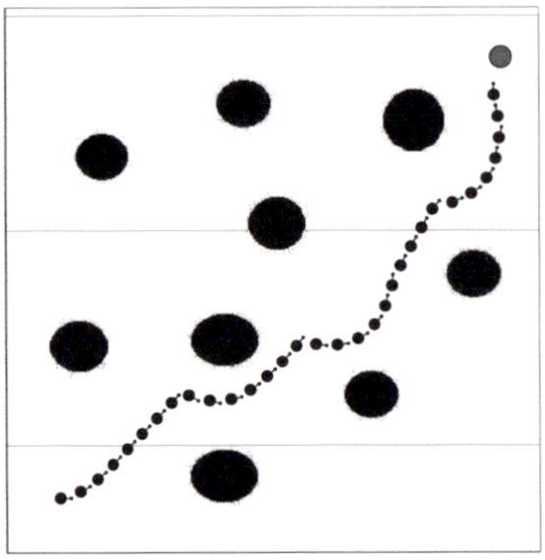

(a) Circular

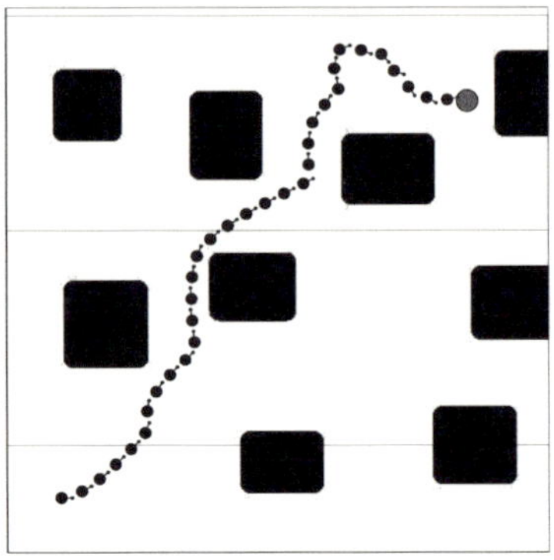

(b) Rectangle

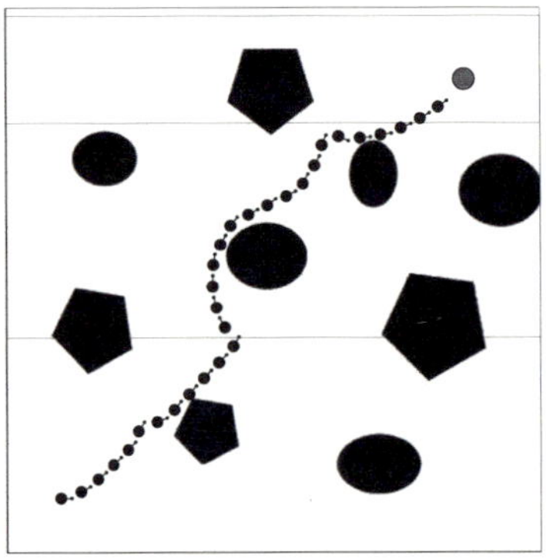

(c) Allotype

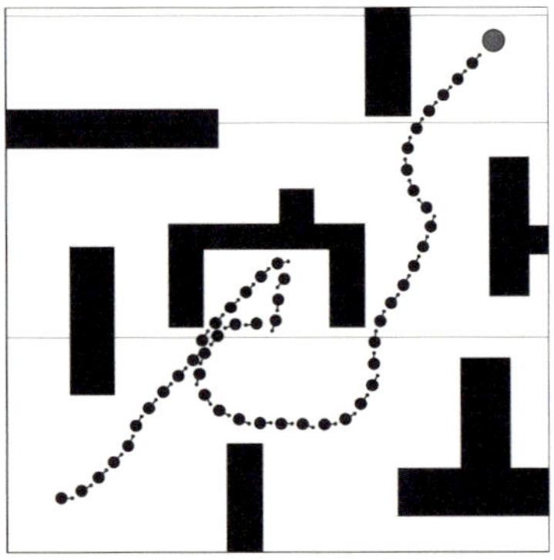

(d) Complicated

Fig. 13. Single Robot Move to the Potential Target with Path Planning

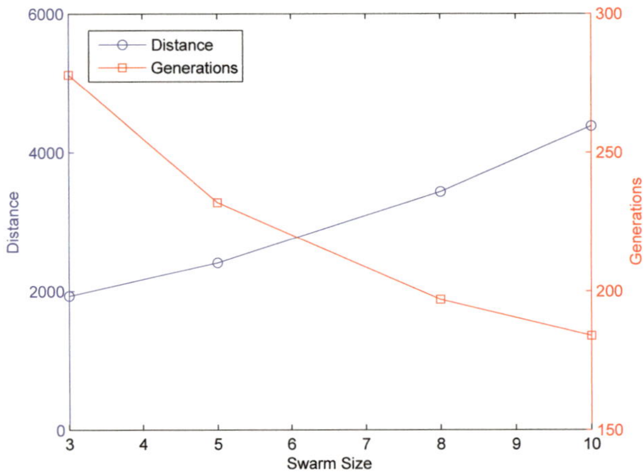

Fig. 14. Relations between Average Distance/Generations and Swarm Size

to decide the best positions on the basis of space-time distribution properties of target and robots. Simulation conducted in closed signal propagation environment indicates the approximate relation between fusion and distance, i.e., the nearer the robot is far away from target, the higher the fusion of signals. Also, a modified artificial potential field method is proposed based on the multiple sensor structure for the space resource conflict resolution. The simulation results show the validity of our sensor-based APF method in the process of search for potential target.

7. References

Bahl P. & Padmanabhan V. (2000). RADAR: An In-Building RF-Based User Location and Tracking System. *IEEE infocom*, Vol. 2, 775-784, ISSN 0743-166X.

Borenstein J. & Koren Y. (1989). Real-Time Obstacle Avoidance for Fact Mobile Robots. *IEEE Transactions on Systems, Man and Cybernetics*, Vol. 19, No. 5, 1179-1187, ISSN 1083-4427.

Campion G.; Bastin G. & Dandrea-Novel B. (1996). Structural Properties and Classification of Kinematic and Dynamicmodels of Wheeled Mobile Robots. *IEEE transactions on robotics and automation*, Vol. 12, No. 1, 47-62, ISSN 1042-296X.

Doctor S.; Venayagamoorthy G. & Gudise V. (2004). Optimal PSO for Collective Robotic Search Applications, *Proceedings of Congress on Evolutionary Computation*, pp. 1390-1395, Vol. 2, 2004.

Ge S. & Cui Y. (2000). New Potential Functions for Mobile Robot Path Planning. *IEEE Transactions on robotics and automation*, Vol. 16, No. 5, 615-620, ISSN 1042-296X.

Hayes A. (2002). *Self-Organized Robotic System Design and Autonomous Odor Localization*, Ph.D. thesis, California Institute of Technology, Pasadena, CA, USA.

Hereford J. & Siebold M. (2008). Multi-Robot Search Using A Physically-Embedded Particle Swarm Optimization. *International Journal of Computational Intelligence Research*, Vol. 4, No. 2, 197-209, ISSN 0973-1873.

Janabi-Sharifi F. & Vinke D. (1993). Integration of the Artificial Potential Field Approach with Simulated Annealing for Robot Path Planning. *Proceedings of the IEEE International Symposium on Intelligent Control*, pp. 536-541, Chicago, USA.

Jatmiko W.; Sekiyama K. & Fukuda T. (2007). A PSO-Based Mobile Robot for Odor Source Localization in Dynamic Advection-Diffusion with Obstacles Environment: Theory, Simulation and Measurement. *IEEE Computational Intelligence Magazine*, Vol. 2, No. 2, 37-51, ISSN 1556-603X.

Khatib O. (1986). Real-Time Obstacle Avoidance for Manipulators and Mobile Robots. *The International Journal of Robotics Research*, Vol. 5, No. 1, 90, ISSN 0278-3649.

Lerman K.; Martinoli A. & Galstyan A. (2005). A Review of Probabilistic Macroscopic Models for Swarm Robotic Systems. *Lecture notes in computer science*, Vol. 3342, 143-152, Springer.

Li D. & Hu Y. (2003). Energy-Based Collaborative Source Localization Using Acoustic Microsensor Array. *EURASIP Journal on Applied Signal Processing*, 321-337, ISSN 1110-8657.

Maalouf E.; Saad M.; Saliah H. & et al. (2006). Integration of A Novel Path Planning and Control Technique in A Navigation Strategy. *International Journal of Modelling, Identification and Control*, Vol. 1, No. 1, 52-62, ISSN 1746-6172.

Marques L.; Nunes U. & de Almeida A. (2006). Particle Swarm-Based Olfactory Guided Search. *Autonomous Robots*, Vol. 20, No. 3, 277-287, ISSN 0929-5593.

Martinoli A. & Easton K. (2002). Modeling Swarm Robotic Systems, *Proceedings of Eighth International Symposium on Experimental Robotics*, pp. 297-306, July 2002, Springer.

Martinoli A.; Easton K. & Agassounon W. (2004). Modeling Swarm Robotic Systems: A Case Study in Collaborative Distributed Manipulation. *International Journal of Robotics Research*, Vol. 23, No. 4, 415-436, ISSN 0278-3649.

Murphy R. (2000). *Introduction to AI Robotics*, MIT Press, ISBN 0262133830, Cambridge, MA, USA.

Ni L.; Liu Y.; Lau Y. & et al. (2004). LANDMARC: Indoor Location Sensing Using Active RFID. *Wireless Networks*, Vol. 10, No. 6, 701-710, ISSN 1022-0038.

Oriolo G.; De Luca A.; Vendittelli M. & et al. (2002). WMR Control via Dynamic Feedback Linearization: Design, Implementation, and Experimental Validation. *IEEE Transactions on Control Systems Technology*, Vol. 10, No. 6, 835-852, ISSN 1063-6536.

Peng J. & Akella S. (2005). Coordinating Multiple Robots with Kinodynamic Constraints along Specified Paths. *The International Journal of Robotics Research*, Vol. 24, No. 4, 295, ISSN 0278-3649.

Pugh J. & Martinoli A. (2006). Multi-Robot Learning with Particle Swarm Optimization, *Proceedings of the 5th International Joint Conference on Autonomous Agents and Multiagent Systems*, pp. 441-448, ACM, New York, NY, USA.

Pugh J.; Segapelli L. & Martinoli A. (2006). Applying Aspects of Multi-Robot Search to Particle Swarm Optimization. *Lecture Notes in Computer Science*, Vol. 4150, 506, Springer.

Pugh J.; Martinoli A. (2007). Inspiring and Modeling Multi-Robot Search with Particle Swarm Optimization, *Proceedings of the 4th IEEE Swarm Intelligence Symposium*, pp. 1-5, Honolulu, HI, USA.

Ren J. (2005). *Applying Artificial Potential Fields to Path Planning for Mobile Robotics and to Haptic Rendering for Minimally Invasive Surgery*, Ph.D. thesis, The University of Western Ontario, London, Ontario, Canada.

Siegwart R. & Nourbakhsh I. (2004). *Introduction to Autonomous Mobile Robots*, MIT Press, ISBN 026219502X, Cambridge, MA, USA.

Singh L.; Stephanou H. & Wen J. (1996). Real-Time Robot Motion Control with Circulatory Fields, *Proceedings of 1996 IEEE International Conference on Robotics and Automation*, Vol. 3.

Warren C. (1990). Multiple Robot Path Coordination Using Artificial Potential Fields, *Proceedings of 1990 IEEE International Conference on Robotics and Automation*, pp. 500-505.

Xue, S. & Zeng, J. (2008). Control over Swarm Robots Search with Swarm Intelligence Principles. *Journal of System Simulation*, Vol. 20, No. 13, 3449-3454, ISSN 1004-731X.

Xue S.; Zeng J. & Zhang J. (2009). Parallel Asynchronous Control Strategy for Target Search with Swarm Robots. International Journal of Bio-Inspired Computation, Vol. 1, No. 3, 151-163, ISSN 1758-0366.

Zou X. & Zhu J. (2003). Virtual Local Target Method for Avoiding Local Minimum in Potential Field Based Robot Navigation. *Journal of Zhejiang University SCIENCE A*, Vol. 4, No. 3, 264-269, ISSN 1673-565X.

Optimization Design Method of IIR Digital Filters for Robot Force Position Sensors

Fuxiang Zhang
Hebei University of Science and Technology
P. R. China

1. Introduction

Digital filtering plays an important role in sensors' signal processing of robots. Not like analog system, it is not limited by parameters of electronic components, so it can process signals of rather low frequency, which is one of its advantages. According to different structure, digital filters can be divided into finite impulse response (FIR) digital filters and infinite impulse response (IIR) digital filters. The output of FIR digital filters only relates with the previous and the present input. Whereas the output of IIR digital filters relates not only with the input but also the previous output. It is to say that IIR digital filters have their feedback. Seen from signal-processing, IIR digital filters have great advantages over FIR digital filters, but they also have their disadvantages at design. The coefficient of IIR digital filters is highly nonlinear, whereas the coefficient of FIR digital filters is linear.

2. Signal processing system of the robot joint force/position sensor

2.1 Configure of the signal processing system

There are two kinds of design methods for IIR digital filters: 1) Frequency translation method, this method has two design routes: one route is first get analog lowpass filter, analog highpass filter, analog bandpass filter and analog band elimination filter by doing frequency band transform to the analog normalized prototype, and then get digital lowpass filter, digital highpass filter, digital bandpass filter and digital band elimination filter by digitization; the other route is first get digital lowpass filter by digitizing the analog normalized prototype, and then get digital highpass filter, digital bandpass filter and digital band elimination filter by frequency band transform in digital domain. 2) Optimization algorithm, it is to design digital filters under certain optimization criterions to get the best performance. Now, there are minimum P-error method, least mean square error (LMSE) method, linear programming method and model-fitting frequency response method etc.
In recent years, some scholars have already applied such intelligent algorithms as genetic algorithm, artificial immune algorithm and particle swarm optimization (PSO) algorithm etc into the design of IIR digital filters and achieved better result. Commonly speaking, filters' capacity is often shown by the permissible error of amplitude characteristic of its frequency response. When designing a filter, we should consider such main technical index as

passband cutoff frequency ω_c , stopband cutoff frequency ω_c , passband toleranceal, stopband tolerance a_2 and passband maximum ripple δ_1, stopband minimum attenuation δ_2,etc. At present, both traditional and optimized design methods need to consider the above mentioned capability index. The author will put forward an optimized design method based on the prior knowledge. According to the method, people only need to know the structure of a filter and to master an intelligent optimization algorithm before finishing the filter's design.

For the signal frequency of the robot joint force/position sensors is rather low, their signal fits to be processed by lowpass filters. There are two kinds of filters: analog filters and digital filters. Here, both analog filters and digital filters are used to process the signals of the robot joint force/position sensors. The configuration of the filters sees Fig. 1.

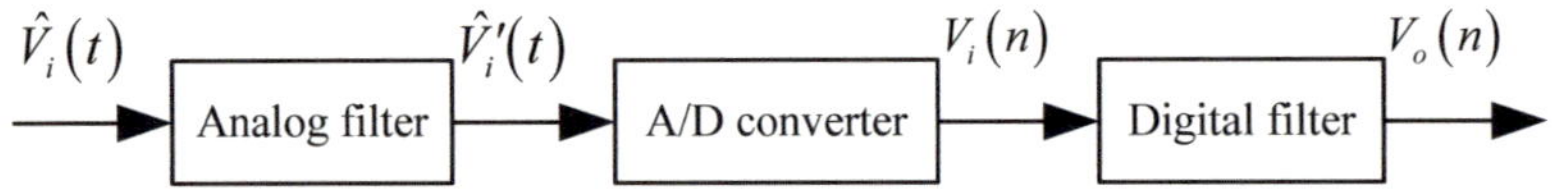

Fig. 1. Configuration of the filters

The output signals of the robot joint force/position sensor are analog input signals $\hat{V}_i(t)$ of the signal processing system. After analog filtering $\hat{V}_i(t)$ were converted to $\hat{V}_i'(t)$, and then $\hat{V}_i'(t)$ were sampled and discretized into input sequence $V_i(n)$ by A/D converter.

2.2 Realization of the signal processing system

(a) Realization of the analog filter

In this research, the sensor signal is magnified by instrument magnifier AD623, and the filter method by double capacitors is adopted which recommended by AD623 user's manual. The schematic of the analog filter is shown in Fig.2.

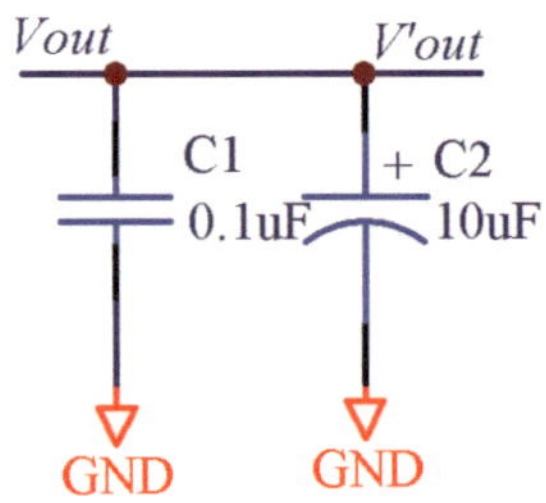

Fig. 2. Schematic of the analog filter

(b) Realization of the digital filter

Generally, the system function of N-order digital filter is

$$H(z)=\frac{b_0+b_1z^{-1}+b_2z^{-2}+\cdots+b_Mz^{-M}}{1+a_1z^{-1}+a_2z^{-2}+\cdots+a_Nz^{-N}} \tag{1}$$

Translating it to difference equation

$$\begin{aligned} y(n)&=b_0x(n)+b_1x(n-1)+b_2x(n-2)+\cdots+a_Mx(n-M) \\ &\quad -a_1y(n-1)-a_2y(n-2)-\cdots-a_Ny(n-N) \end{aligned} \tag{2}$$

Then the digital filter can be realized via Eq. (2).

3. Optimization model of the IIR digital filter of robot joint force/position sensor

The system of IIR digital filter can be shown as Fig. 3

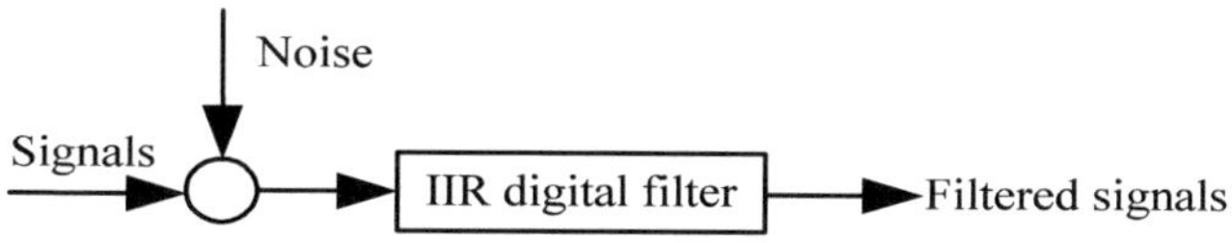

Fig. 3. Schematic diagram of the IIR digital filter

Suppose that the system function of N-order IIR digital filter is

$$H(z)=\frac{b_0+b_1z^{-1}+b_2z^{-2}+\cdots+b_Mz^{-M}}{1+a_1z^{-1}+a_2z^{-2}+\cdots+a_Nz^{-N}} \tag{3}$$

If Eq. (3) is adopted to design IIR digital filter, the number of parameter required optimize is $M+N+1$, and it is difficult to choose the value range of every parameter. Generally, the system function of IIR digital filter is expressed as

$$H(z)=A\prod_{k=1}^{N}\frac{1+a_kz^{-1}+b_kz^{-2}}{1+c_kz^{-1}+d_kz^{-2}} \tag{4}$$

Both Butterworth filter and Chebyshev filter can be denoted as the cascade structural form with second-order unit shown as Eq. (4). When IIR digital filter is denoted by this structural form, the sensitivity of its frequency response to coefficient change is lower. And it is convenient to confirm the value range of every parameter with this structure form.

For robot force/position sensors, its measurement signal is low frequency, generally below 10Hz. And the disturbance is white noise mostly. If power supply is mains supply, the disturbance of 50Hz power frequency would exist. Generally, the analog lowpass filter is used to deal with these kinds of signals. However, it is very difficult to filtering the disturbance of 50Hz power frequency and the low-frequency white noise. If the digital filter is adopted and its cutoff frequency is set rather low, the filter can remove the disturbance of 50Hz power frequency and white noise mostly. From practical experience, it was known that the satisfying effect can be obtained when adopting a second-order lowpass.

The system function of the second-order Butterworth filter can be simplified as

$$H(z) = A\frac{1+2z^{-1}+z^{-2}}{1-cz^{-1}+dz^{-2}} \quad (5)$$

IIR digital filter as a system, the ideal signal after filtered could repeat the input signal perfectly, and with definite system delay. Then the similarity of the actual and ideal output signal would be considered as the evaluation index of filter performance. If the maximum frequency of robot force/position sensor signal is f, and the input signal is simulated with sine function, the function of input signal can be denoted as

$$x(n) = c_s \cdot \sin(2\pi f \cdot n \cdot T_s) + c_{dis} \cdot \sin(2\pi \cdot 50 \cdot n \cdot T_s) + c_w \cdot \mathrm{randn}(1) \quad (6)$$

where c_s is the coefficient of sensor signal, c_{dis} is the coefficient of disturbance of 50Hz power frequency, c_w is the coefficient of white noise, T_s is the sample time of system. randn( ) is the normal distribution random number which represents white noise.
The ideal output after digital filter is

$$y_d(n) = c_s \cdot \sin(2\pi f \cdot n \cdot T_s) \quad (7)$$

The actual output of filter is

$$y(n) = A \cdot x(n) + 2A \cdot x(n-1) + A \cdot x(n-2) - c \cdot y(n-1) - d \cdot y(n-2) \quad (8)$$

Suppose that the delay time is T, the sample size is n, the mean square error (MSE) of IIR digital filter at every sample points can be shown as

$$E = \frac{1}{n-T-1}\sum_{i=1}^{n-T}\sqrt{(y(T+i) - y_d(i))^2} \quad (9)$$

The mathematical model of optimization design of IIR digital filter is

$$\begin{cases} \min E = f(X) \\ s.t. X \in S = \{X | g_j(X) \le 0 \; j = 1, \cdots, m\} \end{cases} \quad (10)$$

where X is optimization variable, $X = \{A, c, d\}$, $g_i(X)$ is restriction function, S restriction region, E optimization aim function, $E = f(X)$.

4. Optimize the parameters of the IIR digital filter using the particle swarm optimization algorithm

4.1 Introduction of particle swarm optimization

Particle Swarm Optimization (PSO) algorithm is a new global optimization evolutionary algorithm invented by Doctor Eberhart and Doctor Kennedy. This algorithm simulates preying of bird. It is outstanding to solve nonlinear optimization problem, and it is simply to realize this algorithm. So it has become an important optimization tool.

In PSO algorithm, the position of particle represents the possible solution. The superiority-inferiority of particle is measured by particle fitness. Firstly, a flock of random particles are initialized. Then the optimal solution is found out via multiple iterating. During every iteration, particle is updated by tracking the two optimal solutions which one optimal solution is found by this particle, namely, individual optimal solution, the other is found by the whole particle swarm presently, namely, global optimal solution.

After found two above-mentioned extremums, particle's velocity and position are updated according to two equations as follow.

$$\boldsymbol{V}_i^{k+1} = w \cdot \boldsymbol{V}_i^k + c_1 \cdot r_1 \cdot \left(\boldsymbol{p}_i^k - \boldsymbol{x}_i^k\right) + c_2 \cdot r_2 \cdot \left(\boldsymbol{p}_g^k - \boldsymbol{x}_i^k\right) \tag{11}$$

$$\boldsymbol{x}_i^{k+1} = \boldsymbol{x}_i^k + \boldsymbol{V}_i^{k+1} \tag{12}$$

where k is generation number, i is serial number of the particle, $\boldsymbol{V}$ is velocity of the particle, $\boldsymbol{x}$ is current position of particle, $\boldsymbol{p}$ is vector form of p_{Best}, g is vector form of g_{Best}, r_1 and r_2 are random numbers from 0 to 1, c_1 and c_2 are learning factors, generally, $c_1=c_2=2$, w is weighting factor, its value from 0.1 to 0.9.

4.2 Improved algorithm

(a) During the basic PSO algorithm search in solution space, the particle would oscillate round global optimal solution at later period. To solve this problem, the improvement can be done as follows: with iteration going, to let velocity update the weighting factor, the weighting factor decreases from maximum $w_{\max}$ to minimum $w_{\min}$ linearly, namely

$$w = w_{\max} - \frac{w_{\max} - w_{\min}}{G_{\max}} \cdot G \tag{13}$$

where G is generation number of current iteration, $G_{\max}$ is total generation number of iteration.

(b) To make the PSO algorithm search in solution space and to ensure convergence rate, the position space and velocity space of particle need to be limited. Eq. (5) will to be

$$x_{\mathrm{r}} = \left(x_{1\min}, x_{1\max}, x_{2\min}, x_{2\max}, x_{3\min}, x_{3\max}\right) \tag{14}$$

$$v_{\mathrm{r}} = \left(v_{1\min}, v_{1\max}, v_{2\min}, v_{2\max}, v_{3\min}, v_{3\max}\right) \tag{15}$$

4.3 Parameters coding and the choice of the fitness function

To solve X using PSO algorithm, the optimization variable X should be coded, to become particle of PSO algorithm. According to characteristics of PSO algorithm, parameters can be denoted with real number. To every particle of filter shown in Eq. (5), if the current position of particle is denoted with $\boldsymbol{X} = \{A, c, d\}$, and the velocity is denoted with $\boldsymbol{V} = \{V_1, V_2, V_3\}$, then the coding structure would be adopted as follows:

A, c, d	V_1, V_2, V_3
Position of the particles	Velocity of the particles

PSO algorithm confirms the superiority-inferiority of particle's current position via fitness. So the fitness function must be chosen according to the practical demand. Here Eq. (9) is chosen as the fitness function of IIR digital filter design. Evidently, the less the value of E is, the less the mean square error of filter parameter $\boldsymbol{X}$ corresponding this particle is. Then this particle is corresponding to the better coefficient of filter. When the algorithm finished, the particle with the minimum fitness during the whole running period is the optimal solution obtained by this algorithm, namely, filter parameter.

4.4 Optimization steps

(a) Set parameters of PSO algorithm, including population size S_{pop}, dimension S_{dim}, weighting factor w, position space x_r, velocity space v_r.
(b) Set parameters of IIR digital filter, such as c_s, c_{dis}, c_w, T_s, *etc.*
(c) Initialize the particle swarm, to randomly initialize every particle's position and velocity in parameter space.
(d) Solve the system delay time, and to calculate the particle's fitness according to Eq. (9).
(e) Initialize the current particle's position as individual extremum $\boldsymbol{p}_{Best}$, and the position of particle with minimum fitness among all individual extremum as g_{Best}.
(f) Update the particle's position and velocity according to Eq. (14) and Eq. (15).
(g) Solve the system delay time, and to calculate the particle's fitness again.
(h) Judge whether to update the particle's individual extremum $\boldsymbol{p}_{Best}$ and the global extremum g_{Best} of particle swarm.
(i) Repeat step (f) to (h), till meeting precision demand or reaching iteration times pre-set.
(j) Output gBest, and to obtain the coefficient of IIR digital filter.

5. Results and analysis

To prove the validity of optimization design method of IIR digital filter for robot force/position sensor presented in this paper, an optimization program was completed in the Matlab 6.5 circumstance and several simulation experiments were made. In these simulation experiments, Parameters of the PSO algorithm were set as: swarm size $S_{pop} = 50$, parameter dimension $S_{dim} = 3$, minimum weighting factor $w_{min} = 0.1$, maximum weighting factor $w_{max} = 0.9$. According to former design experience, the value range of every filter coefficient are as: $x_r = [0.00001, 0.01, 1, 2, 0.00001, 1]$, maximum velocity $v_r = [-0.005, 0.005, -0.5, 0.5, -0.5, 0.5]$, sample time $T_s = 0.02$ s, maximum frequency of sensor signal $f = 0.05$ Hz, signal amplitude $c_s = 1.5$, disturbance amplitude of 50 Hz power frequency $c_{dis} = 0.1$, amplitude coefficient of white noise $c_w = 0.15$, simulation time $t = 50$ s.
Fig. 4 is the variety course of every generation's fitness of PSO algorithm.

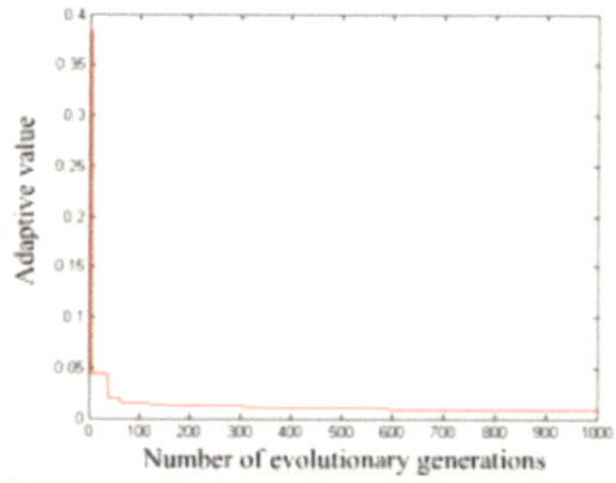

Fig. 4. Curves of unfiltered and filtered signals of the robot force/position sensors

Fig. 5 a) and b) are the signal curve of robot force/position sensor before and after filtering respectively. The last parameters of IIR digital filter are set as A = 0.0064, c = 1.5186, d = 0.5439, delay time T = 0.36 s, MSE E = 0.0091. From Fig. 4 b), we can know that the filter effect is perfect for sensor signal of f = 0.05 Hz.

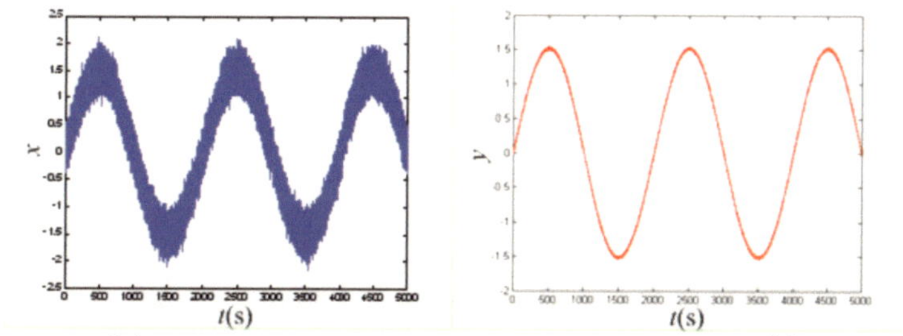

Fig. 5. Curves of unfiltered and filtered signals of the robot force/position sensors, (a) is curve of unfiltered signals, (b) is curve of filtered signals.

The frequency response optimized is

$$H\left(e^{T_s j\omega}\right) = 0.0064 \times \frac{1 + 2e^{-0.02 j\omega} + \left(e^{-0.02 j\omega}\right)^2}{1 - 1.5186e^{-0.02 j\omega} + 0.5439\left(e^{-0.02 j\omega}\right)^2} \quad (16)$$

From Eq. (16), the amplitude-frequency characteristics curve of filter designed in this research can be obtained, as shown in Fig. 6.

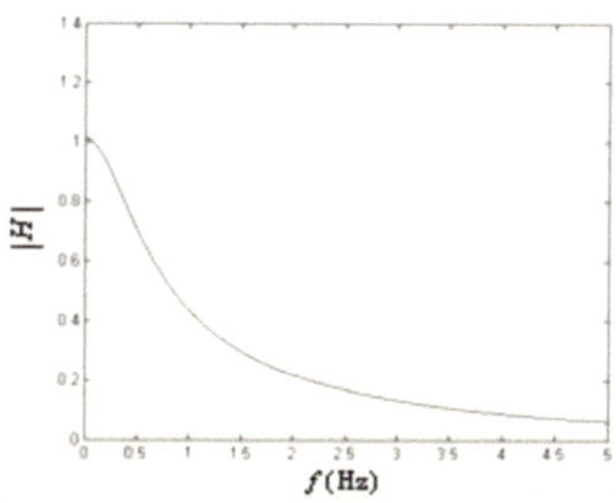

Fig. 6. Magnitude-frequency characteristics curve of the filter

From Fig. 6, it can be seen that signal is attenuated under 0.1, when its frequency decreased to 5 Hz. So the filter can remove the disturbance of 50 Hz power frequency and white noise mostly.

6. Conclusion

Aimed at the design of IIR digital filters of robot force/position sensors, a design method is put forward. Its optimization principle is the minimum MSE between ideal and actual output signal at time-domain. And the mathematics model aiming at second-order Butterworth lowpass filter was set up. This method needn't understand the complicated design theory and method for digital filter and the characteristic of filter, such as passband frequency, cutoff frequency, passband attenuation, ripple, etc. This method only requires the understanding of the structure characteristic of filter and the maximum frequency of sensor signal. Thus the parameters of the filter can be optimized in a suitable intelligent optimization method. An optimization program of the PSO algorithm was developed in the Matlab circumstance. The result of simulation experiment proves the validity of this method, and to be strongly practicable.

7. References

Cheng, P. Q. (2007). *Digital Signal Processing Tutorial 3rd edition*, Tsinghua University Press, ISBN 9787302139973, Beijing, P. R. China

Chen, J. & Xu, L. H. (2006). Road-Junction Traffic Signal Riming Optimization by an Adaptive Particle Swarm Algorithm, *Proceedings of the 9th International Conference on Control, Automation, Robotics and Vision (ICARCV'06)*, pp. 1-7, ISBN 1424403421, Singapore, Dec. 2006

Chen, W. S. & Zhao, J. (1999). *Computer Control of Mechatronic System*, Harbin Institute of Technology Press, ISBN 9787560313979, Harbin, P. R. China

Hou, Z. R. & Lv, Z. S. (2003). Particle Swarm Optimization Algorithm for IIR Digital Filters Design. *Journal of Circuits and Systems*, Vol.8, No.4 , (Apr. 2003) 16-20, ISSN 007-0249

Kalinlia, A. & Karaboga, N. (2005). Artificial Immune Algorithm for IIR Filter Design. *International Journal of Artificial Intelligence*, Vol.18, No.8 , (Aug. 2005) 919-929, ISSN 0974-0635

Karaboga, N., Kalinli, A. & Karaboga, D. (2004). Designing digital IIR filters using ant colonyoptimisation algorithm. *Engineering Applications of Artificial Intelligence*, Vol.17, No.6 , (Jun. 2004) 301-309, ISSN 0952-1976

Li, X.; Zhao, R. C. & Wang, Q. (2003). Optimizing the Design of IIR Filter via Genetic Algorithm, *Proceedings of IEEE International Conference on Neural Networks for Signal Processing*, pp. 476-479, ISBN 0-7803-8177-7, Nanjing, China, Sep. 2003

Seo, J. -H., Im, C. -H, Heo, C. -G., Kim, J. -K., Jung, H. -K. & Lee, C. -G. (2006). Multimodal Function Optimization Based on Particle Swarm Optimization. *IEEE Transactions on Magnetics*, Vol.42, No.4, (Apr. 2006) 1095-1098, ISSN 0018-9464

Shi, Y. & Eberhart, R. C. (1998). A Modified Swarm Optimizer, *Proceedings of the IEEE International Conference of Evolutionary Computation*, pp. 69-73, Anchorage, USA, May. 1998

Tang, K. S., Man, K. F., Kwong, S. & Liu, Z. F. (1998). Design and Optimization of IIR Filter Structure Using Hierarchical Genetic Algorithms. *IEEE Transactions on Industrial Electronics,* Vol.45, No.3, (Mar. 1998) 481-487, ISSN 0278-0046

Ting, T. O., Rao, M. V. C., Loo, C. K. & Ngu, S. S. (2003). Solving Unit Commitment Problem Using Hybrid Particle Swarm Optimization. *Journal of Heuristics,* Vol.9, No.6, (Jun 2003) 507-520, ISSN 1381-1231

Wu, B., Wang, W. L., Zhao, Y. W., Xu, X. L. & Yang, F. Y. (2006). A Novel Real Number Encoding Mechod of Particle Swarm Optimitation for Vehicle Routing Problem, *Proceedings of the 6th Congress on Intelligent Control and Automation*, pp. 3271-3275, ISBN 7810778021, Wuxi, P. R. China, Jul. 2006

Zeng, J. C., Jie, J. & Cui, Z. H. (2004). *Particle Swarm Optimization*, Science Press, ISBN 7030132548, Beijing, P. R. China

6

Visual Analysis of Robot and Animal Colonies

E. Martínez and A.P. del Pobil
Robotic Intelligence Lab, Jaume-I University Castellón, Spain
Interaction Science Dept., Sungkyunkwan University, Seoul, S. Korea

1. Introduction

Micro-robotics calls for the development of tracking systems in order to study the movement of each micro-robot in a colony to answer questions about **what** they are doing and **where** and **when** they act (see Fig. 1). Moreover, micro-robots can be used to emulate social insect behaviour (Camazine et al., 2001) and study them through tracking experiments involving several miniature robots on a desktop table. Thus, principles of self-organization in these colonies, which were studied so far by analysis of a tremendous amount of insect trajectories and manual event counting, are now better understood by biologists thanks to robotics research.

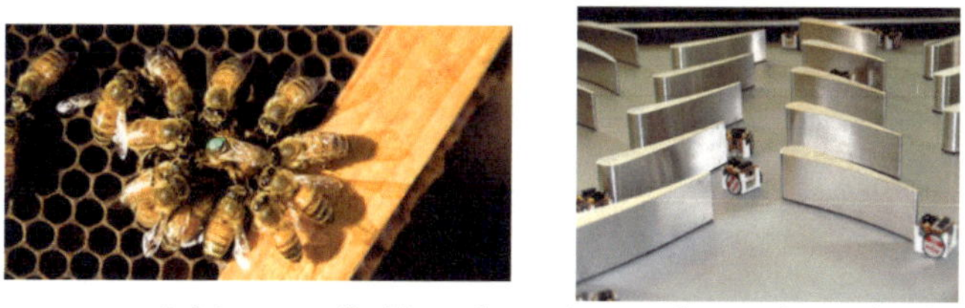

Fig. 1. Analogy between social insects (left) and a micro-robot colony (right)

Although this approach is only recently increasing its popularity, computer vision systems for tracking moving targets are widely used in many applications such as smart surveillance, virtual reality, advanced user interfaces, motion analysis and model-based image coding (Gavrila, 1999). Surveillance systems seek to automatically identify people, objects or events of interest in different kind of environments (Russ, 1998; Toyama et al. 1999; Haritaoglu et al., 2000; Radke et al., 2005). However, this problem is not easy to solve. First of all, it is not viable to tag each colony member under study. On the one hand, the tag selection process can be difficult since tags must be very small in some cases and, therefore, it might not be possible to detect them in an image. Furthermore, tags can become ambiguous when a swarm is composed of many individuals. On the other hand, tagging can alter individual behaviour. So, an application for tracking unmarked object has been developed. A new problem arises: how to identify the same object in two consecutive *frames*. SwisTrack (Correll et al., 2006) is a previous work following this approach which we try to improve. It is a platform-independent, easy-to-use and robust tracking software developed to study robot swarms and behavioural biology. It is part of the European project LEURRE (http://leurre.ulb.ac.be.2006) focused on building and controlling mixed societies composed of animals and artificial embedded agents. In preliminary case studies towards this aim (Caprari et al., 2005), an Insbot team has been introduced into a swarm of cockroaches and allowed for modification of the natural behaviour of the swarm. We will show that our application achieves robust performance in object identification and tracking without the need of a strong intervention by the user.

As the structure of the designed method (see Fig. 2), this paper is organized as follows: the visual segmentation and detection of objects are described in Sec. 2 and 3. In Sec. 4 we outline the tracking problem and its solution. Experimental results are given in Sec. 5 and discussed in Sec. 6.

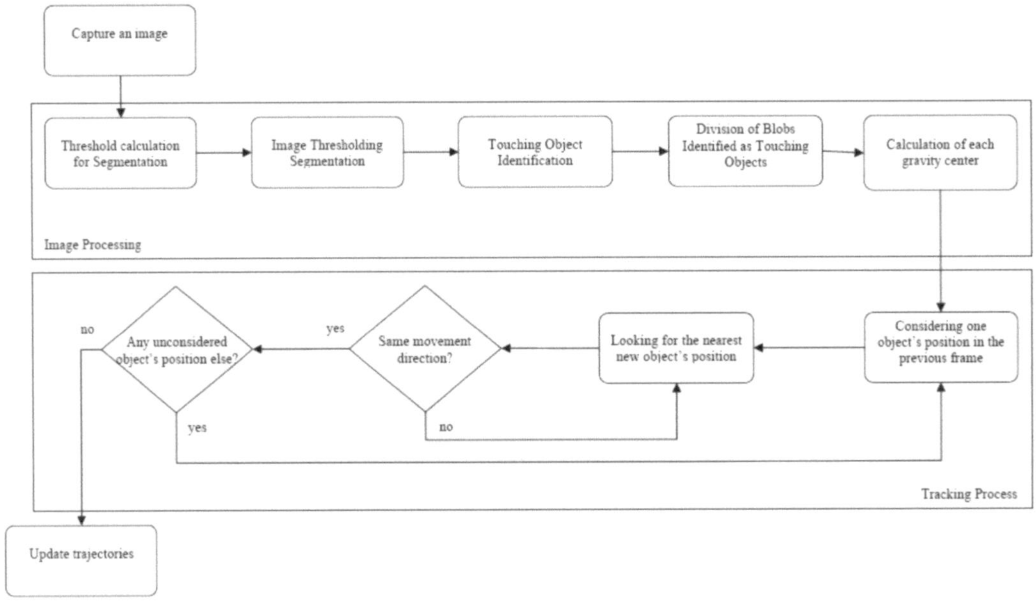

Fig. 2. Flowchart of the whole designed method

2. Object Segmentation

A common element of any surveillance systems is a module that is capable of identifying the set of pixels which represents all the individuals under study in each captured image. There are several techniques to carry out this task. For example, the background modeling approach (Toyama et al., 1999; Haritaoglu et al., 2000) allows to model dynamic factors such as blinking of screens, shadows, mirror images on the glass windows or small variations in illumination due to flickering of light sources. Pixels are classified as background or foreground depending on the fitting of their values with the built model. As a drawback, this method is not capable of adapting to sudden illumination changes, and we ruled it out with the aim of developing a more robust surveillance application in the presence of variation of lighting conditions. On the other hand, most of the alternative techniques are developed by gray-level image processing so that if available images are in color, it is necessary to convert them to gray-level. As our system has color images as input, the binary image resulting from the segmentation process can be obtained from a combination of three

binary images (each color channel generates a gray-level image which is segmented by the selected method obtaining a different binary image), or from a gray-level image obtained directly from the color one.
Thus, the first step is to convert the captured color image to a gray-level one. For such preprocessing, the Hue-Saturation-Intensity (*HSI*) system is used since it encodes color information by separating an overall intensity value *I* from two values encoding *chromaticity* - hue *H* and saturation *S*. *HSI* might also provide better support for computer vision algorithms because it is amenable to normalization for lighting and focus on the two chromaticy parameters that are more associated with the intrinsic character of a surface rather than the lightning source. Thus, the resulting gray-level image is only built from the *intensity* value. Derivation of *HSI* coordinates from *RGB* coordinates is a common process in computer vision (Shapiro and Stockman, 2001).
Once the gray-scale image is available, a segmentation process has to be applied on it. Although frame difference is the easiest and fastest method to detect moving objects in an image, it fails when the objects are steady. This problem could be solved by taking a reference image with no objects and subtracting it from the new ones. Nevertheless, a little illumination change might make the whole process fail, thus, an alternative algorithm should be chosen. In our case, the corresponding binary image is obtained from an input gray-scale by thresholding operations as in *Swistrack*. This technique defines a range of brightness values in the original image: pixel value greater than a threshold (or lower, depending on its definition) belongs to the foreground and the rest of pixels are classified as background. The drawback of this method is the correct determination of the threshold. In *Swistrack* two different kinds of reference images are used, depending on the mode in which the system is operating:

- **Static background**: the background image is captured at the beginning of the experiment and is not updated at any time;
- **Running average**: the reference image is built as the running average of all video *frames* processed until that moment

The threshold is fixed in both cases and represents the minimum difference required to classify a pixel as foreground. It is important to note that the fixed threshold is sensitive to changes in lighting conditions, especially in the first operation mode in which the reference image is not updated during all the experiment. Although the running average is more capable of dealing with illumination changes, it might consider objects that stop moving for a long period of time as part of the background, without detecting their presence in the scene. We have implemented a method for automatically calculating the threshold based on histogram properties by updating its value in each frame, in order to adapt it to variations of the lighting conditions. This provides an advantage over the *Swistrack* method, as significant intensity differences between the objects to be tracked and the background are not necessary.
After the threshold setting, two consecutive morphological operations are applied on the binary image resulting from the segmentation process. These steps are required to erase isolated points or lines caused by different dynamic factors such as, for example, changes induced by camera motion, sensor noise, non-uniform attenuation, blinking of lights or atmospheric absorption. A 3x3 erode filter is used to delete these artefacts and then a 3x3 expand filter is applied to recover the foreground region. A result of the whole process can be observed in Figure 3, where a group of micro-robots is seen from above. As it can be seen,

although the lighting conditions are not good in some places, the designed application is capable of detecting all visible micro-robots in the image. However, the pixels due to light reflexions on the arena are not removed from the image. This issue will be solved by means of the implemented labeling method described in next section.

Fig. 3. An image captured by the system camera (left), the binary image obtained by the segmentation process (center) and the resulting binary image after applying two morphological operations (right)

3. Object Identification

The aim of this stage is to obtain a labeled image in which each label identifies one colony member. This can be a difficult task when objects are touching one another, because an identified *blob* contains all objects with, at least, one point in common. The method implemented to achieve the above goal can be divided into three steps:

1. Labeling of the identified *blobs* in the input binary image. A row-by-row labeling method (Shapiro and Stockman, 2001) is used to reduce the computational cost of the whole process. The binary image is scanned twice: the first time to tag each foreground pixel based on the labels of its neighbors and to establish equivalences between different labels; the second, crossed scan, will unify tags which belong to the same *blob*
2. Classification of the labeled *blobs* as targets to be tracked or as bad-segmented pixels, and detection of collisions inside a *blob* identified as a tracking target. All targets are assumed as not touching in the first captured image. The number of targets to be tracked is specified by the user, and the application calculates the minimal and maximal size allowed from the first captured image. This knowledge, together with the number of the detected *blobs* in each frame, allows to define a series of criteria to determine when a *blob* represents more than one object, and to reject all *blobs* that do not identify target objects but are instead the result of a bad segmentation, as it occurs with the set of noisy pixels in the example of Fig. 3
3. Segmentation of *blobs* that represent groups of more than one object to be tracked. This step is explained in more detail in the next section

As seen above, it is possible that the same *blob* identifies more than one object to be tracked. Thus, it is important to detect these situations and split up the *blob* in the corresponding objects. There are two different tasks to be performed: determining the number of touching objects inside the same *blob* and splitting them up.

The first goal is achieved through several criteria which are relationships between *blobs* and object sizes. They can be easily set up by the application, assuming that no target objects are touching in the first captured image. Thus, our application calculates the maximum and

minimum dimensions of the visual objects from the first captured scene and the criteria remain set. This step is important because perceived object size can vary with the distance between the arena and the camera and if an object size in pixels is directly related to its real size, as in *Swistrack*, a calibration error can be introduced in all calculations. Due to this error, the application might fail the tracking process. So, the only parameter our application needs, which is requested to the user, is the number of objects to be tracked.
The next step is to split up the different objects which compose one *blob*. As it is difficult to identify several objects at the same time, we have studied three different, possible situations assuming that only two objects are touching. Thus, our application split up any complex *blob* in two different parts: one target object and another *blob* which can be again composed of more than one micro-robot. If the new *blob* represents several micro-robots, the split-up process is recursively applied until the obtained *blob* is composed of only one target object. The three different cases that have been studied are the following:

1. two objects touching only in one point;
2. two objects sharing one side, that is, they are horizontally or vertically aligned;
3. two objects touching in several points which do not correspond to their sides

In the first case, a contour method is used. A chain code is calculated by considering that the contact pixel will be visited twice. The method takes into account the contour irregularities due to the segmentation process and it applies different criteria to determine the correct contact point as shown in Fig. 4.

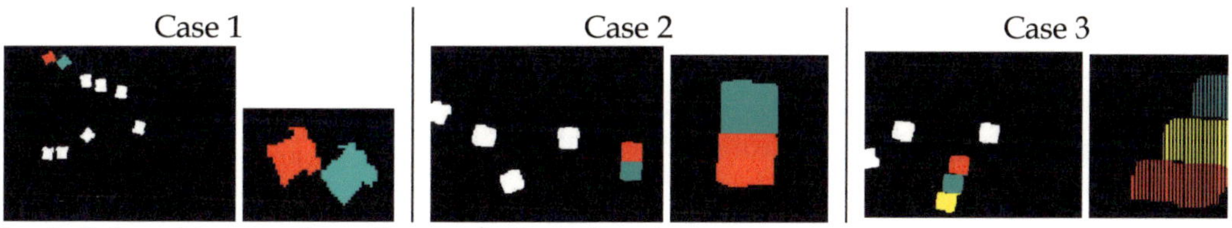

Fig. 4. Colored images from the resolution of contact cases

The second case, when two objects share one side, has been considered because of the micro-robots used in our experiments, the *Alice*2002 (Caprari and Siegwart, 2005) (see Fig. 5). These micro-robots can be seen from above as boxes and two *Alice*2002 can share one side in any moment. It is important to note that this case does not apply to micro-robots that do not have a shape in which a side can be shared. A method based on dimension criteria is used to determine the common side, and it estimates their splitting line as shown in Fig. 4.

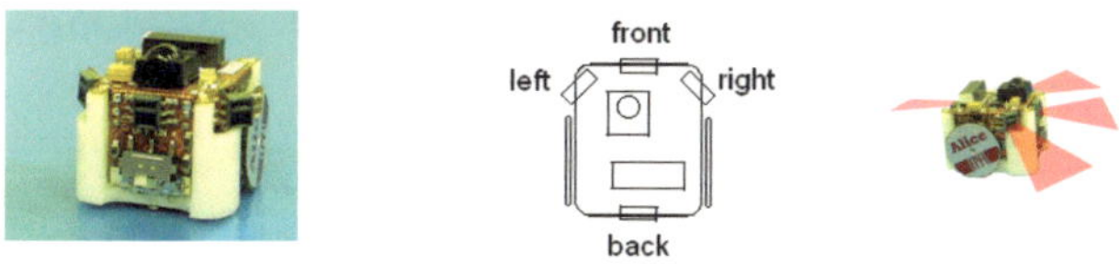

(a) A micro-robot *Alice* 2002 (b) Infrared proximity sensors

Fig. 5. Micro-robot *Alice*2002

Finally, the most general and complex case is when an object and another *blob* compose a bigger *blob*, and the contact between them is through several pixels which do not correspond to an object side. Therefore, the designed method is based on holes inside *blobs*. Again, this might be the result of a bad segmentation. For this reason, a set of criteria were defined for detecting when a hole is due to bad segmentation and when it is a hole between two different objects. As it can be seen in Fig. 4, the designed method provides successful results.

4. Tracking Micro-robots

Once each micro-robot is identified as an object, the next step is to match each object with one of those detected in the previous frame, in order to obtain its trajectory.

Object position can be calculated as the geometrical center of gravity of object contour (Correll et al., 2006), but we decided to calculate it as the geometrical center of gravity of a *blob* corresponding to an object. Since the correspondence between an object and a *blob* has been obtained in the previous step, this procedure is easier and faster. The issue now is how to associate each center of gravity with its corresponding object between the new ones. The chosen solution, the *nearest neighbor* method, is an easy one, but its implementation raises several issues (Correll et al., 2006). The different way of dealing with them will determine the successfulness of the application.

The first challenge to solve is the case of an object that is closer to the previous position than the real one (situation already described in a previous work (Correll et al., 2006)). A quadratic assignment problem for minimizing the sum over the distance of all assignments is used in *Swistrack*, but this does not constitute an optimum solution since it fails in some cases. On the contrary, a solution focused on the previous movements of objects is presented here, that is, the matching algorithm associates the information on the nearest neighbor with that regarding the previous movement direction.

It might also be that an object disappears from the scene (Correll et al., 2006), but if the application does not detect all elements specified by the user, then it will fail when this situation occurs, because objects enter or leave the arena, and the system will repeatedly capture another image until it finds all the objects. Another situation (again presented in (Correll et al., 2006)) is when two shared trajectories are divided at the wrong time, but this is not possible in our application because *blobs* are divided into their corresponding objects even though they are touching, as previously explained. Finally, an additional skill of our application is the ability of avoiding un-associated contours.

Overall, our application is capable of solving the four different situations expounded in (Correll et al., 2006) and does not need the help of the user for correcting wrong trajectories.

It is also important to note that the modified nearest neighbor technique is only applied on a small region of the image, not on the whole image, in order to make the application faster. Again, it is not possible to fix the search area size because a delay can be produced during capture process. Thus, our application calculates the search area dimension based on capture time between *frames* and the maximum velocity of tracking objects, which will be requested to the user. This reduces the computational time and guarantees the success of the matching process.

5. Experiments

We first provide a brief overview of the robotic platform used, followed by the experimental results.

The experimental setup is depicted in Figure 6. A camera is pointing downwards to the desktop where the micro-robots are working. Our application operates with monocular color video images (see Fig. 6). The distance between the camera and the arena can vary from one setup to another and the system calculates the parameter values needed for obtaining the different criteria. It is important to note that the background of the micro-robot workspace is black in all our experiments, while the most common solution is to use a white background.

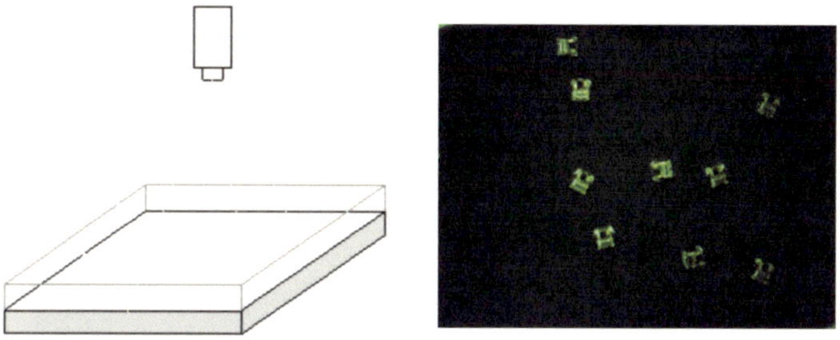

Fig. 6. Experimental setup (left) and a 320x240 captured image by the camera (right)

The objects to be tracked are *Alice*2002 robots, as mentioned above. They are extremely sensitive to external forces and can be very easily damaged if not handled with care. Among their features, we can mention:

- tiny dimensions (22 mm (width) x 21 mm (length) x 20 mm (height))
- small weight (aproximately 11 g)
- infrared proximity sensors (front, right and left) to avoid obstacles
- low consumption (12 - 17 mW)
- autonomy (up to 10 hours thanks to its Ni-MH rechargeable battery (Varta 3/V40H))
- velocity of 40 mm/s

Finally, a Graphical User Interface (GUI) has been developed to check the performance of our application. It is composed of two different windows (see Figure 7(a)): on the left, the user can observe the images taken in real-time and, on the right, a graphical window is showing the different positions of the objects. Each obtained trajectory is drawn in a different color to help the user identify each target. As the duration of the experiments is unknown and the amount of points can be considerable, the application only shows the last seventy object positions to ease tracking of each described trajectory to the user.

Two different experiments have been carried out. The first one is the tracking of three unmarked *Alice*2002 (see Figure 7). Six untagged *Alice*2002 are studied in the second experiment (Fig. 8). Both experiments have been carried out at different times of the day and in different days to test the robustness of our application to different lighting conditions.

As it can be seen in Fig. 7a, all micro-robots to be tracked are not touching in the first stage. Thus, our application can obtain the information it needs: the objects position, i.e., their geometrical center of gravity, and the maximum and minimum size allowed for any object. For clarity of representation, objects are highlighted by inscribing them in circles.

Although there are relevant delays between the first and the second *frames* and between the second and the third ones, our application is capable of correctly tracking the objects as shown in Fig. 7b.

To check the system in different situations, we have changed the moving pattern of the objects during the experiment. For the first 25 *frames* all three objects are describing a

clockwise circular trajectory. A different circular trajectory with smaller radius is described during the next 25 *frames*, as shown in Fig. 7d. Finally, the micro-robots are set in wall following mode, so they describe a straight-line trajectory until they find a wall to follow, as can be observed in Fig. 7e.
The second experiment was similar. In this case, our application had to track six unmarked *Alice*2002. Again, the first captured *frame* (see Fig. 8a) reveals that the experiment starts without collisions between objects. The trajectories described in this experiment are, first, the smallest-radius circular trajectory; then, four of the micro-robots change their trajectory describing a circular trajectory with a larger radius and the two remaining ones go straight ahead looking for a wall to follow. Now, two more micro-robots change to the wall following mode. It is important to note that our application is capable of detecting objects only partially visible as shown in Fig. 8d.

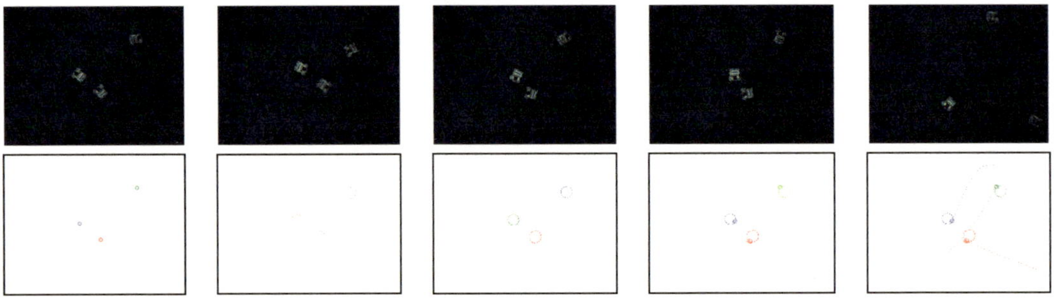

(a) Initial State (b) After 5 frames (c) Circular trajectory (d) Circular trajectory with a different radius (e) Following wall mode

Fig. 7. Three *Alice*2002 tracking experiment: captured image (up) and trajectory image (down)

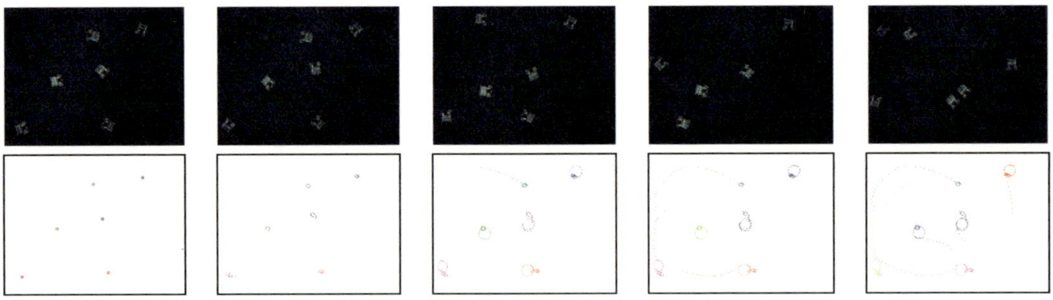

(a) First Stage (b) Circular Trajectory (c) Change in some trajectories (d) Another change in some trajectories (e) Following wall mode

Fig. 8. Six *Alice*2002 tracking experiment

In addition, examples of the use of our split-up method are finally shown in Fig. 9. A one-shot video segment of 10 minute duration is available at
http://www.robot.uji.es/lab/plone/Members/emartine

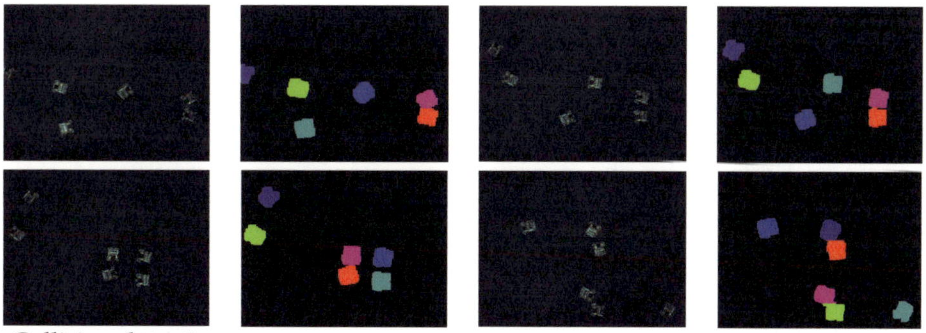

Fig. 9. Collision detection

To conclude this section, a graph is presented (see Fig. 10) which compares the trajectory followed by a member of the studied colony in a multiple-target experiment versus the trajectory obtained by the developed software. As it can be observed, there is no mismatch in data-association thanks to the implemented method to split up blobs when several members are in touch.

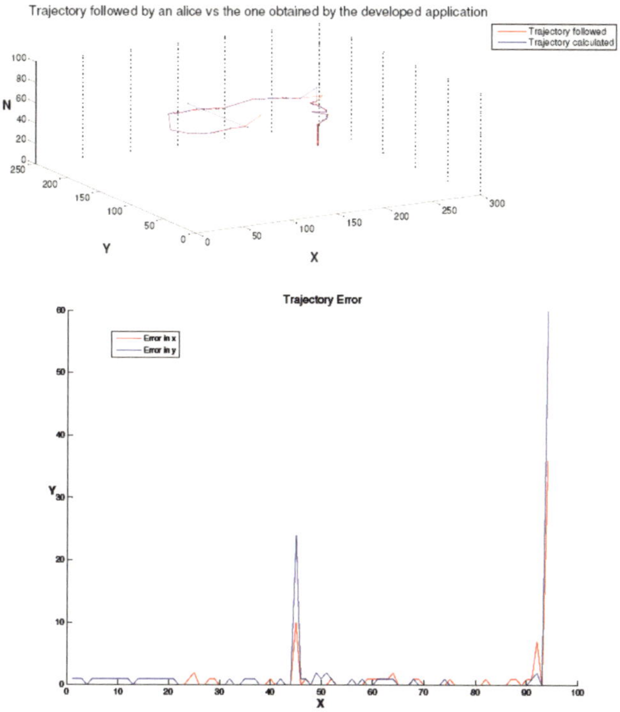

Fig. 10. Trajectory followed by a single target vs individual trajectory obtained by the implemented software (above) and error (below)

6. Conclusions

We have presented a tracking application to study micro-robots or social insect cooperative behavior without the risk of conditioning the results by tagging them. Our system has been compared with previous ones, and namely with *Swistrack*, an application intended to control mixed societies. Although this previous study had the same goal, the authors deal with the tracking problem in a different way. The given results have shown the robustness of our application with regard to lighting conditions. Also, no special illumination is required and performances do not depend on the surrounding objects, as for example it occurs in *Swistrack*.

Our designed method also solves situations in which there are several objects touching one another and it can match an object position in one frame with its position in the next frame. It is also capable of detecting objects even though their velocity is very slow or if they do not move, a case typically difficult for similar methods.

As a further achievement, our application only requires two parameters from the user: the number of target objects and their maximum speed. No thresholds need to be set manually.

Overall, we have designed an application transparent to the user who does not need to know the implementation details to work with it.

So far, our application has only been tested with homogeneous robotic societies. As further research, we plan to test it with mixed societies.

7. Acknowledges

This research was partly supported by the Korea Science and Engineering Foundation under the WCU (World Class University) program funded by the Ministry of Education, Science and Technology, S. Korea, Grant No. R31-2008-000-10062-0), by the European Commission's Seventh Framework Programme FP7/2007-2013 under grant agreement 217077 (EYESHOTS project), by Ministerio de Ciencia e Innovacion (DPI-2008-06636, DPI2004-01920 and FPI grant BES-2005-8860), by Generalitat Valenciana (PROMETEO/2009/052) and by Fundacio Caixa Castello-Bancaixa (P1-1B2008-51)

8. References

Camazine S.; Deneubourg J.L.; Franks N.R.; Sneyd J.; Theraulaz G. and Bonabeau E. (2001). Self-Organization in Biological Systems. *Princeton Studies in Complexity,* Princeton University Press

Caprari G.; Colot A.; Siegwart R.; Halloy J. and Deneubourg J.L. (2005). Building mixed societies of animals and robots. *IEEE Robotics and Automation Magazine,* 12, 2, (58-65)

Caprari G. and Siegwart R. (2005). Mobile micro-robots ready to use: Alice, *Proceedings of IEEE/RSJ International Conference on Intelligent Robots and Systems,* pp. 3295 – 3300

Correll N.; Sempo G.; Lopez de Meneses Y.; Halloy J.; Deneubourg J.L. and Martinoli A. (2006). Swistrack: A tracking tool for multi-unit robotic and biological systems, *Proceedings of IEEE/RSJ International Conference on Intelligent Robots and Systems (IROS),* pp. 2185-2191

Gavrila D.M. (1999). The visual analysis of human movement: A survey. *Computer Vision and Image Understanding,* 73, 1, (82–98)

Haritaoglu I.; Harwood D. and Davis L.S. (2000). W4: Real-time surveillance of people and their activities. *IEEE Transactions on Pattern Analysis and Machine Intelligence*, 22, 8, (809 - 830)

Toyama K., Krum J., Brumitt B., and Meyers B. (1999). Wallflower: Principles and practice of background maintenance, *Proceedings of the Seventh IEEE International Conference on Computer Vision*, volume 1, pp. 255 - 261, Kerkyra, Greece

Radke R.J.; Andra S.; Al-Kofahi O. and Roysam B. (2005). Image change detection algorithms: A systematic survey. *IEEE Transactions on Image Processing*, 14, 3, (March), (294-307)

Russ J.C. (1998). *The Image Processing Handbook*, CRC Press, third edition

Shapiro L.G. and Stockman G.C. (2001). *Computer Vision*, Prentice Hall, NJ